S. R Hendren

The Indians of Colonial Virginia

A Study of their Institutions and Social Culture

S. R Hendren

The Indians of Colonial Virginia
A Study of their Institutions and Social Culture

ISBN/EAN: 9783337154400

Printed in Europe, USA, Canada, Australia, Japan

Cover: Foto ©Suzi / pixelio.de

More available books at **www.hansebooks.com**

THE INDIANS OF COLONIAL VIRGINIA

A STUDY OF THEIR

INSTITUTIONS AND SOCIAL CULTURE.

----

by

S. R. Hendron

Contents.

Page

Introduction   1

Chapter 1.

Virginia and its Indian Inhabitants - Tribal Divisions and Numbers - Languages - "Confederacies" - Physical, Mental and Moral Characteristics - Dress - Ornaments. - - - - - - p.11

Chapter 11.

Dwellings - Furniture - Towns - Family and its Character - Kinship through Females - Courtship - Marriage - Domestic Life - Children, their Training and Education - Pocohontas, a Title of Endearment - Food: Hunting and Fishing - Division of Time - Cultivation of the Ground: Agriculture - Preparation of Corn for Food: Bread - Cookery - Food in General and its Varieties - Drink - - - - - - - - - - - -p.31

Chapter 111.

Trade and Commerce - "Money" - Ingenuity in "Handicrafts" - Bows and Arrows - Shields and Swords - Knives - Boats - Work in Shell - in Stone - Metal-Working - Pottery - Weaving - Spinning - "Engraving" - Tannery - Musical Instruments - Dancing - Songs - Games - "Arts" - Medicine - Physicians or "Medicine-men" - Mantic Art - "Prophecies" - Traditions - p.50

Chapter 1V.

Character of Government - Extent of Powhatan's "Empire" - Powhatan's Residences - His Personal Appearance - Character - His "Imperial" State, Privileges and Immunities - Nature of the Empire - Tenure of Land - Werowance and Cockarouse - Councils - "Laws" of the Indians - Organization of "Shiers" - Duties, Privileges, Immunities of the "Officials Priests and their Influence - Councils - Character of the so-called Powhatan "Confederacy" - Social Structure - War and Military Matters - Treatment of Captives - Treaties, Embassies and Triumphs - "Foreign Relations" of the Virginia Indians - Internal Relations - Conduct required at Council General Summary -p.85

Chapter V.

Character of Religion - Temples - Dualism - Worship of the
"Devill" - Belief as to the Great God - Burke's Opinion -
Beverley on the Religion of the Indians - Strachey on the
Same - Immortality of the Soul - Worship of Manibozho or
Shawondose - The "Great Hare" - Hariot on the Religion of
the Virginia Indians - The Soul after Death - Byrd on the
Religion of the Virginia Indians - Embalming - Great Temple - Priests. Their Manner of Treating the Sick, their
Functions - Atlas - Holy Days - Feasts - Smith on Conjuration or "Pawawings" - Hariot on the Same - Whitaker on
their "Magic and Sorcery"- Beverley on Same - Functions of
Conjuror - Objects of Worship: Fire - Water - Thunderstorm-
Sun - Cardinal Points or Four Winds - Human Sacrifice -
Huskanaving - Conclusion - - - - - - - - - - - - - - - p.115

Chapter VI.

Indian Survivals - Words - "Tribes" - Descendants of Pocohontas - Indian Place-Names - Indian Summer - - - - - -p.156

Bibliography - - - - - - - - - - - - - - - - - - - -p.164

Introduction.

It is a real misfortune that so little attention was paid to the early settlers of Virginia to the manners, customs, laws and language of their Indian neighbors. For, although it is true that a critical and scientific examination of their dark-skinned neighbors could not, from the nature of things, be expected from these hard-pressed colonists, yet, it might reasonably be anticipated that we should have had a more complete account given us of that interesting race of "Virginians" which blossomed out in such remarkable characters as the stern and haughty old "Emperour" Powhattan and that mild and lovely character - his daughter Pocahontas Matoaca.

Smith, the Father of the Colony and the historian of young Virginia, it might have been expected, would have given us more than he really did do in this regard, but it is probable that as a man of deeds rather than words, he had little leisure for so doing. Notwithstanding, however, the fact that his account is brief and cursory, it is far from contemptible, giving, as it does, some of the most important information to be had on the subject in hand. The titles of this author's works* having to do with our sub-
- -
* In the citation of Smith's works in this monograph, I have made use of Ed. Arber's edition of his works.

ject are:

(1) "A Map of Virginia with a Description of the Countrey, the Commodities, People, Government and Religion", etc.- published in 1612, and

(2) "The Generall Historie of Virginia, New England and the Summer Isles" especially the first, second and third books which are indeed a reprint with variations of number (1). This book first appeared in 1624.

Stith*, writing about 1747, and dealing with Virginia History from 1585-1624, strangely speaks not at all upon this subject, and Beverley** who writes about 1705, while he gives some space to this theme, still leaves us with the impression that he is much too superficial. "He appears," says the historian Burk***, on this occasion to feel a portion of zeal, and to display some of the talents essential to such an investigation. But his zeal is but the hectic of a moment, and he soon relapses into his former apathy."

Of course there were several other writers who give some account of these Indians valuable and instructive, and their extreme value must be acknowledged; but, in general, it cannot but be admitted with reference to all such au-

----
* History of Virginia.
**   "   "   "   edition of
*** "   "   "   1, 310 -

thors that the neglect of all opportunity for gaining information concerning this remarkable people, when that information was readily to be gained, can now only to a certain extent, be repaired. What can be done, however, is to make the best of all the contemporary accounts and the numerous references to these Indians in non-contemporaneous authors and scientific writers, by comparing them, eliminating or reconciling their apparently contradictory statements, and then by collecting and collating these numerous references and extracts to form therefrom an accurate and complete picture of the institutions and social culture of the Virginia Indians; and this I have endeavoured to do as far as possible by the use of original authorities, but supplementing their often scrappy and superficial accounts by a careful study of their kindred and neighboring tribes.

However, though difficult be the subject and the authorities scattered, and, it must be confessed, rather unsatisfactory in some of their most important details, there are writers whose accounts are, in spite of their atrocious style and verbiage, highly valuable; and by the careful, painstaking and judicious use of each and every one of them having at the same time reference to the customs and practices of kindred tribes, we can not fail in coming to conclusions which if not of extreme interest, will be, from

the antiquarian standpoint, at least, of the highest importance and value. To resume, then, a consideration of our authorities: Besides the accounts of Smith and Beverly are others of extreme importance. The account of William Strachey is such an one. This was published originally in volume sixth of Hakluyt's Voyages, but as early as 1849 it was published separately, being edited by R. H. Major under the auspices of the Hakluyt Society of London. It consists of "two bookes" with the first of which we have chiefly to do. The title tells the rest:

"The Historie of a Travaile into Virginia Britannia, explaining the Cosmographie and Commodities of the Countrey Together with the Manners and Customes of the People:- Gathered and observed as well by Those who went First Thither, as collected by William Strachey, Gent. Three years thither Imployed Secretarie of State, and of Counsaile with the Right Honorable the Lord La Ware, His Majestie's Lord Govenour and Capt. Generall of the Colonie" etc. Date about 1612.

Of about equal importance, though brief in compass is the work of another contemporary authority - one, who, in fact, lived years among the Indians, became thoroughly acquainted with their curious manners and customs, and who was on one occasion saved from a cruel death at their hands

by that "guardian angel" of the Virginia colony - Pocahontas - finally, however, meeting his end during the Massacre of 1622 was Henry Spelman, described as "third son of the antiquary Sir Henry Spelman." His account is called "a Relation of Virginia," and from its pages important information concerning many curious ceremonies, rites, institutions, laws, etc. are to be drawn. It has been reprinted from the original manuscript by Mr. Edward Arber in his edition of Captain John Smith's works (mentioned above) forming one large volume in the English Scholar's Library.

In this volume, too, and likewise in Purchas His Pilgrimes (quod supra) iv. 1685-90, is contained another valuable source of information, which, while not giving, nor claiming to give any description of the Indians, still, as ore-bearing earth, contains nuggets of valuable information. This is Master George Percy's Account of the Discovery and Settlement, etc., etc.

In volume IV of Archaeologia Americana, pp.40-65 is to be found edited by Rev. E. E. Hale the "Relatyon of the the Discovery of our Rivers,"etc., by Captain Newport from 25 May - 22 June, 1607, by an anonymous writer, who, by the general consensus of the opinion of learned authorities is "Captain Gabriell Archer." There is also in this, probably by the same author a short "Description of the People"

Of not quite the importance and value for our subject as the above mentioned works, being, as it probably is, largely based on them, is that celebrated collection entitled Purchas His Pilgrimage and Purchas His Pilgrimes, published about 1612. The religious observances of the Virginian Indians are herein especially dealt with.

In as much as the Indians with whom the early colonists of Virginia came into contact were very closely related both in race, institutions and language to those of whom we are informed in De Bry's illustrations and Hariot's account. I have thought good to make use of their works and the accounts of the other voyages to Roanoke in a somewhat critical and comparative way. The full title of Hariot's account is:-

"A Briefe and true Report of the New-found-Land of Virginia" by Thomas Hariot. This is published in vol. iii of Hakluyt, pp. 324-341. It is published also in De Bry's collection of Voyages entitled "Brevis Narratio, etc. The illustrations by De Bry and Wythe are of especial value, and are reproduced in Beverly and Strachey. Another work of especial value just here is Lawson's History of Carolina of the date 1714, afterwards plagiarised by Brickell in his Natural History of North Carolina -(1737).

For the same reason that the Indians of Roanoke Isl-

and and the neighborhood are noticed, the Indians of southern Maryland must demand some degree of attention; and furthermore because of the fact that many of these latter Indians belonged to the Powhatan "Confederacy" which as is well known, extended to the Patuxtent river. In this regard the "Relatio Itineris in Marylandiam" of Father White supplies quite a store of information; also the chapters on the Maryland Indians in Scharf's History of Maryland and Bozman's Maryland, especially volume I.

Jefferson's Notes on Virginia in volume VIII of his collected works (also printed separately) pp.148-175, treat in brief form of the Virginia Indians-(1781); and numerous interesting notices of the Virginia Indians are given in Byrd's Westover Manuscript, published in two volumes at Richmond in 1846. Rev. Hugh Jones' work on the "Present State of Virginia"(date about 1724) is likewise of great value; while some of Rev. Alexander Whitaker's letters to friends in England and his "Good News from Virginia" (1613) are of some importance.

Alexander Brown's "Genesis of the United States", containing, as it does, reprints of the most invaluable contemporary manuscripts upon Early Virginia history, must be extensively used by any one who undertakes a study of colonial Virginia from whatever point of view - consequent-

ly it is of high value for us.

Among other works that have been used in the preparation of this monograph, though of course their accuracy and thoroughness must always needs be verified by a comparison with the original authorities, if possible, are:-

(1) Campbell's History of Va. c.VI. pp. 84-92.

(2) Burke's   "   " " vol. iii. c.I. pp.5-91, also vol. I. pp. 309-314 (Appendix)-

(3) Cooke's History of Virginia, c.   (in Amer. Commonwealth's series)-

(4) Neill's Va. Carolorum, London Co. of Va. & Va. Vetusta - which like Alexander Brown's "Genesis" contain valuable reprints of manuscripts relating to this subject.

(5) Howe's Historical Collections of Va.

(6) C.C.Jones' Antiquities of the Southern Indians. This work, however, deals mainly with the antiquities of the Georgia Indians; only by allusion to those of the Virginia Indians.

(7) Morgan's Ancient Society. An excellent work, chiefly having to do with the Iroquois and kindred tribes, but especially valuable as giving an insight into the general principles of Indian government and civilization in general.

(8) H.R.Schoolcraft's Archives of Aboriginal Knowledge, 6 vols.

(9) H.R.Schoolcraft's League of the Iroquois.

(10) Drake & Heckewelder have both written works of extreme value on the North American Indians in general; and, finally, I should mention various articles in

(11) The Encyclopedia Britannica (ninth edition) as being worthy of careful attention.

To be added to the above enumeration, are such invaluable aids to research into the manners, customs, etc.,etc. of the aborigines of North America as:

(1) Publications of the Bureau of American Ethnology in 4 volumes; and

(2) Annual Report of the Bureau of American Ethnology,

(3) Proceedings of the American Ethnological Society.

(4) "   "   "   "   Anthropological " from 1887-1893, and finally, Field's Indian Bibliography gives a conspectus of the whole field of literature having to do with aboriginal knowledge. The works enumerated have been quite extensively used in the preparation of this monograph, though, of course, some to a greater ex-

tent than others. On the other hand, I have omitted to mention many I have used because they would be, more properly indicated in foot-notes.

The method I propose to follow in developing the institutional and cultural side of the Indians of Colonial Virginia is as follows : I shall discuss in order:

(1) Their Habits, Numbers, Language, Personal Appearance, Character, etc.
(2) Their Domestic Economy, Private Life, Family, Agriculture, Food, Shelter--
(3) Their Commerce, Handicrafts, Music, Songs, Diversions, Writing, Medicine, etc.
(4) Their Governmental Institutions and Their Ruler.
(5) The Religious Institutions and Beliefs, and finally,
(6) Indian Survivals in Virginia at the present day.

Chapter I.

THE INDIANS OF VIRGINIA: Habitat, Numbers, Language, Appearance, etc.

The extent of country now forming the State of Virginia consists of high-land and low-land; the south-eastern part, having an area of 23,000 square miles, is a broadly undulating plain, rising from the sea-coast to an altitude of from 100-800 feet, while the north-western portion consists of successive mountain ranges running nearly parallel across the state from north-east to south-west, separated by parallel valleys (800-1200 ft. alt.) [1] This geographical division of the State should be noted; for, in the consideration of the tribes of Colonial Virginia, our attention will be limited to those inhabiting the south-eastern and eastern portions of the State, in as much as in Colonial times, Virginia west of the Blue Ridge was uninhabited by any tribes as a permanent residence or abode, but was frequented by the Indians only in the capacity of wandering hunters or warriors. This portion of the state was, indeed a place of combat for warring tribes to the north and south of it, [2] and so will have no place in a consideration of

---
(1) For the topography of Virginia see Maj. Hotchkiss' article in the Encyclopedia Britannica, art. "Virginia"-
(2) See Withers' Border Warfare, p.39; Kercheval Hist. of the Valley, c.2.

the Indians of Virginia. It is to the eastern portion of
Virginia that our attention must be directed: the inhabitants of this country - the main and characteristic branch
of the "Ancient Virginians"- will demand consideration in
this monograph.

According to Captain John Smith [1] that portion of
Virginia, which lies between the sea-coast and the mountains, and extends from the Potomac to the southern waters
of the James [2] - the Isenacommacah [3] of the natives - was
inhabited by forty-three different tribes of Indians.
Thirty of these were united into a grand, patriarchal "empire" or "confederacy" [4] under the great "Emperour" Powhatan: the thirteen remaining tribes going to form the two
separate but mutually allied "confederacies" called by the
names of their dominant tribes the Mannahoacks and Manakins [5] ("People of the Sword").

The dominions of this august and mighty chief Powhatan, long the most important rival and implacable foe
with whom the English settlers in America ever came into
contact, extended over that portion of the country south of

----
(1) Smith: Generall Historie, Bk.2., pp. 347-352; Strachey, ch.2.
(2) Embracing Tide-water and Midland Virginia.
(3) See Strachey, p. 47.
(4) There was no such thing as a "confederacy" in Virginia. see infra, pp. 98,99, 113.
(5) Also spelled Monacans.

the Potomac between the sea-coast and the falls of the rivers together with the Eastern Shore, embracing, consequently, an area of about 8000 square miles and a population capable of putting into the field 2,400 warriors, that is to say, about 8,000 souls.(1) The thirty "nations" or individual components of the Powhatan "Confederacy" had in 1609 habitat and warrior-population as follows:-(2)

1. The Tauxenents of Fairfax with 30 warriors
2. The Patowomekes "(King George and Stafford) 200 "
3. The Cuttatawomens of (King George and Richmond) 20 "
4. The Pissassecs of (King George and Richmond) - "
5. Onawmanients of Westmoreland 100 "
6. Rappahanocks " Richmond Co. 100 "
7. Moraughtacunds of (Lancaster and Richmond) 80 "
8. Secacaonies of Northumberland 30 "
9. Wighcocomicos of " 130 "
10. Cuttatawomens of Lancaster 30 "
11. Nantaughtacunds of (Essex and Caroline) 150 "

---

(1) Using the ordinary ratio (3:10) of able bodied males to whole population.
(2) See Strachey, pp.35-40; Smith, Generall Hist., bk.2, pp.346-357, Burke's Virginia, iii, 89; Jefferson's Notes, pp.136-140, etc. In addition to the tribes given above and mentioned by Spottswood (1711) were the Stuckarocks, Totteros, Saponies.

12. The Mattapamients of Mattapony river with 30 warriors
13. " Pamunkies of King William with 300 "
14. " Werowocomicos of Gloucester " 40 "
15. " Payanketanks of Payanketank river with 55 "
16. " Youghtamunds " Pamunkey river with 57 "
17. " Chickahomanies of Chickahominy river -250 "
18. " Powhatans)
19. " Arrohatocks) of Henrico Co. 40 "
20. " Weanocs of Charles City with 100 "
21. " Paspaheghs of James City " 40 "
22. " Chiskiacs of York " 45 "
23. " Kecoughtans of Elizabeth City with 20 "
24. " Appamatucks of Chesterfield with 60 "
25. " Quiocohanoes of Surrey with 25 "
26. " Warrasqueakes of Isle of Wight with
27. " Nasamunds of Nansemond with 200 "
     (1)
28. " Chesapeakes of Princess Anne with 100 "
29. " Accohanocs of Accomac with 40)Eastern
) Shore
30. " Accomacs of Northampton with 80)tribes

Besides this powerful "confederacy" and virulently hostile to, and leagued together against it were two other so-called "confederacies". i.e., those of the Mannahoacks and Man-
----
(1) See Forrest: Historical and Descriptive Sketches of
    Norfolk, p.36.

skins.[1] The former consisted of eight tribes: viz, the Whonkenties and Tauxitanians dwelling in Fauquier, the Hassinungaes and Tegninaties in Culpepper, and the Ontponies in Orange, who inhabited the country between the Potomac and Rappahanock; while the three tribes remaining: the Stegarakies of Orange, the Shackakonies of Spottsylvania, and the Mannahoacks[2] of Spottsylvania and Stafford dwelt between the Rappahanock and York rivers. The third "confederacy"- the Manakins - consisted of five tribes: viz, the Manakins[3] of the upper James, and the Manasiccapanoes of Fluvania and Louisa dwelling between the York and James; the Monahassanoes of Buckingham and Bedford, the Massinacacs of Cumberland, the Mohemenchoes of Powhatan occupying the country between the James and the present North Carolina line. It is evident, then, from a glance at the map that, for the most part, the Manakins inhabited the country between the James and York rivers above the falls of these rivers; while the Manahoack "confederacy" occupied that portion of the state lying between the Rappahanock and York rivers and the country drained by the head-waters of the

----
(1) Later known as the Tuscaroras, see Bancroft: Hist. of U.S., vol.   p.
(2) These Mannahoacks were the chief tribe to whom the other seven paid tribute: Smith. Map of Va. p.71.
(3) These Manakins were the chief tribe to whom the other seven paid tribute: Smith, Map of Va. p.91 and Strachey, p.104.

Potomac and Rappahanock rivers.

Not only, however, were the Mannahoacks and Manakins opposed to the Powhatans geographically and politically, but there was a considerable dissimilarity in their respective languages: for, as has been admitted by all proficients in Indian linguistics and philology. While the Powhatans and their subject tribes belonged to the Algonkin family,(2) the other two "confederacies" belonged to the Huron or Wyandot-Iroquois (3) linguistic and ethnical group of the North American aborigines.(4)

Several "languages"(i.e., dialects) as many as eleven different are mentioned by Captain Smith(5) as being spoken by the native Indians that environed Powhatan's terri-

---

(1) E.g. such authorities as Drake, Morgan, Schoolcraft, Heckewelder, Trumbull: indeed no one opposes this view.
(2) The Algonkin family spoke a language, which, says Bancroft, (ii. pp.394,395) "was heard from the Bay of Gaspe to the Valley of the Des Moines; from Cape Fear, and it may be, from Savannah to the land of the Esquimaux; from the Cumberland river of Kentucky to the southern branches of the Mississippi. It was spoken through a country that extended through 60° of longitude and 30° of latitude." See also Encyclopedia Britannica, vol.I. pp. 686-693.
(3) Including the Hurons, Oneidas, Onondagas, Cayugas, Senecas and others.
(4) There were seven great linguistic and ethnical groups:
    (1) the Algonkin, (2) the Iroquois, (3) the Mobilian,
    (4) Dakotah and Sioux, (5) Cherokee, (6) Catawba and
    (7) Shoshonee.- See also Encyclopedia Britannica, art. on "America", vol.I. pp. 686-693.
(5) Generall Historie, bk.2. p.351, also Description of Virginia, p. 55.

tories; viz., the "languages" of the Chowanokes, the Mangoags, the Manakins, the Mannahoacks, the Massawomees, the Powhatans, the Susquesahanoughs, the Atquanachuks, the Tockwoughs and Kuscarawaokes; and, so great was the dissimilarity between them that we are told by the same authority interpreters had to be employed in conferences between them. Still, we are informed by Beverley,(1) that though these languages differed very much between themselves, yet there was a sort of general language(2) - that of the Occaneeches (whoever they were)- in use among all the tribes in Virginia like the Latin of the learned in Europe or the "lingua franca" spoken in the Levant.

Besides these "confederacies" and speaking languages (dialects) of the Iroquois type were the Nottoways on the Nottoway river and the Meherrins and Tutelogs on the Mehewin river, who were, Jefferson thinks, connected with the Chowances of North Carolina.(3) By the consensus of learned authorities, the Meherrins and Nottoways belong to

------

(1)) History of Va. p.148. Strachey says of the Virginia)-Indians that "spoke likewise more articulate and plain.
(2)) and some more inward and hollowe"- p.63.
(3) Same as Shawnee from Shawano = "South". See Schoolcraft V. 409 and Waitz iii, p.24.

the Wyandotte-Iroquois group. Says Bancroft, following such authorities, "the Chowanoes, the Meherrins and the Nottoway villages of the Wyandotte family have left their (i.e. Wyandotte-Iroquois) names to the rivers along which they dwelt."[1]

To give some idea of the linguistic relations existing between the Algonkin language and that spoken by the Powhatans on the one hand, and between the Nottoway dialect and the Iroquois on the other, the parallel column of the numerals[2] in these several languages (given below) will be sufficient. Always bearing in mind the important fact that such similarity is not confined to the numerals alone, but is evident by the entire structure of the respective languages. Here is the table:-

Numerals	Algonkin[3]	"Virginian"[4]	Oneida[3]	Nottoway[3]
1	payjik	necut	anscot	nute
2	ninch	ningh	daganee	dekance
3	nissoo	nuss	hason	arsa
4	nayoo(y)	yough	kaiyalee	kentag
5	nahran	paranske	wisk	whisk
6	ningootwassoo	comotinch	yahyah	oyag
7	ninchwassoo	toppawoss	judak	ohatog
8	nissowassoo	nissawash	takalon	dekra
9	shongassoo	kekatough	wathin	deheerunk
10	metassoo	kaskeke	oyalee	waha

(1) Bancroft's Hist of U.S., ii. p.40
(2) For a Dictionaire of the Ind. Lang." see Strachey, p. 180-196; Smith Gen. Hist. bk.2, p.380-384.
(3) Proc. of Amer. Ethnol. Soc. ii. P/106-115; Hall's Indian Vocabulary, pp. 78-139.; Schoolcraft, League of the Iroquois, pp.392-400.
(4) See Vocab. in Smith's Gen. Hist. bk.2, pp.381-383

The specific character or distinctive features of these Virginia Indian dialects were, it may safely be affirmed, those of all the Algonkin and Iroquois dialects in general; viz, they were of the incorporative, polysinthetic or agglutinative type, words being condensed and built up by the introduction of ideographic roots, subjoined or prefixed to which were tensal, pronominal or other appendages variant as describing varying objects or relations. Again, they observed the all-prevailing rule (sc. in Indian Languages) that every animate verb requires an animate subject and vice versa, and as a consequence of this usage all sex distinction (grammatically speaking) in these tongues is obliterated. Some other characteristics to be noted in these dialects might be mentioned, such are,

1. Their great powers of geographical description. especially Proper Names.
2. Their use of pronouns as inseparable prefixes both to verbs and nouns.
3. Their indiscriminate use of nouns as verbs and verbs as nouns.
4. The prevalence of mouth-sounds among them of Hebrew "aleph" and "yoth"
5. Their ample provision for denoting number .
6. Their peculiar inflexion of words, changing their

.form,

       a - for locality,

       b - for general quality,

       c - to express hurtfulness or the reverse

       d - to express   diminutives -

7. Their use of inseparable particles as prepositions.

8. Their possession of many sounds and idioms unknown to the English, and vice versa [3]

    The population of Ancient Virginia was comparatively small. Though from a glance at the number of tribal names, we might hastily assume the presence of a large and thickly settled population, yet when we examine more closely into the matter, we find that far from such being the case the population was exceedingly sparse and thinly scattered. For instance, we are informed by Smith [1] that within a radius of sixty miles from Jamestown as a center there were only about 5,000 people: of these 1500 were warriors. This was likewise the case on the Eastern Shore where Master Jno. Pory tells us there were only about 2,000 souls.[2] In fact the density of the population of the Powhatan confederacy was only about one to a square mile, or roughly

----

(1) Smith, General Hist. bk.2, p.360; Map of Va. p.65; Stith, p.91.
(2) in Smith's Gen. Hist. bk.4, p.570.
(3) For general Characteristics of the Ind.lang's see Du-

speaking about one fortieth of the present average density
of the population. (1)

The complexion of the Virginia Indian was dark brown or chestnut, a color deepened by the free use of bear's grease, "red-tempered oyntments" and exposure to the weather; for, while in youth their complexion was fair, as they (2) grew older, a gradual but decided darkening of its color took place. Their hair was coal-black and coarse like a (3). (5) horse's mane, straight and long, though few wore beads; (5) their cheek-bones high, their nose broad and flat, their lips "bigg", their mouths large and their eyes a brilliant black and full of animal fierceness and ferocity, an ex- (6) pression rendered yet more frightful by an averted gaze and a sort of squint: in fine, love of vengeance and lawless (7) license stood forth in every feature. In physical develop- (8) ment, the Virginia Indian was tall, erect and admirably proportioned; fit model for Polycletus or Lysippus, Praxiteles or Polygnotus. With thews and sinews hardened by con-

----
(1) Using the ratio 3:10
(2) Smith says they were "born white." see also Beverley,
    Hist. of Va. pp.127,128.
(3) See Purchas V.843; Father White, p.39; Strachey, p.63;
    Ed.Ma: Wingfield's Acc't.
(4) Percy (in Browne's Genesis of the U.S.1,162) mentions having seen a "yellow-haired Virginian".
(5) Strachey, p64; Smith Gen.Hist.bk.2.p.361. see also Smith
    Gen.Hist. bk.3, p.464.
(6) Howe's Col's of Va. p.139; Strachey, p.64.
(7) Beverley: Hist. of Va. p.140

tinual exercise and exposure and rendered supple by the free
use of oil, he was active and agile.[1] In fleetness of
foot,[2] he could outstrip the bear or run down the buck or
elk; and such were his powers of endurance, that he could
bivouac under the leafless trees of the forest in the frost
and snow of mid-winter with scarce a fire,[3] or travel for
weeks at a time with little or no food.[4] The women were
as a general rule, smaller in stature than the men, beautiful, with a well-formed figure, pretty hands, clear-cut
features and a soft, sweet voice.[5]

So general was this fine physical condition that
Beverley[6] says no such thing could be found among the Virginia Indians as a crooked, bandy-legged, dwarfish or otherwise mis-shapen person; though, perhaps, this fact might
be attributable to a free use of the Spartan remedy (i.e.,
the exposure of deformed children): if such was the case,
certain it is, they spared the old men; for we meet with
----
(1) Their capacity for seeing and smelling was remarkable, see Byrd, ii. 281.
(2) Jones, Present State of Virginia, p.9; Archaeologia America, pp.40-55, and Howe's Historical Collections of Va. pp. 137-138.
(3) Smith's Gen.Hist. bk.2, p.361; Strachey, p.68; Beverley, p.142.
(4) Beverley, p.142.
(5) See Strachey, p.64. "When they sing" he says, "they have a pleasant taunge in their voyces".
(6) Hist. of Virginia, p.146.

some remarkable instances of longevity among these Indians recounted by various authors notably Percy (1) and Archer (2).

In character the Virginia Indian was fickle, treacherous, inconstant, crafty and rather timorous (3), quick of apprehension and in their rude fashion quite ingenious. Some, of course, were bolder - less fearful than others - but all without exception were prudent and wary. Once in danger, however, he was calm, composed and stoically indifferent to torture; equally inflexible, stern and immovable - a true "Stoic of the Wood" (4). In conversation, he was modest, dignified and unassuming; in peace, lazy, listless and indolent; in war, vengeful, treacherous and bloodthirsty, never forgiving nor forgetting an injury (5). Though hospitable (6), they were covetous and so rather thievish (7); but they never stole from friends, and were by nature affable

----
(1) In Brown's Genesis of the United States, I, 165. c Campbell, pp. 90, 91.
(2) See Archaeologia Americana IV., 55.
(3) Whitaker "Good Newes from Virginia" in Brown 2, 585.
(4) Campbell, pp. 90, 91.
(5) See Beverly. Hist. of Va., p.179 and compare with famous remark of John Randolph of Roanoke.
(6) See numerous quaint and interesting accounts of Indian hospitality in Smith, Hariot, Hakluyt's Voyages, Churchill's Voyages, Harris's Voyages, etc.
(7) Percy in Brown I, 162; Smith. Generall Historie, bk.2, p. 361.

and liberally disposed. In fine, they were "most quiette, lovinge and faithfull, voide of all guile and treachery and such as lived after the manner of the golden age". (1)

(2) John Esten Cooke graphically portrays the character of the Virginia Indian as "not at all resembling the savages of other lands; tall in person, vigorous, stoical, enduring pain without a murmur; slow in maturing revenge, but swift to strike; worshipping the lightening and thunder as the flash of the eyes, and the stern voice of their unseen god; without piety, passionately fond of hunting and war; children of the woods with primitive impulses; loving and hating inveterately, a strange people".

(3) Though improvidence is a fault frequently ascribed to Indian character in general, it certainly cannot be laid to the account of the Virginia Indian; for history assures us that the stores of corn habitually hoarded by them in their granaries, (4) in numerous instances saved the colonists from perishing. (5) In this regard, Master John Pory (6) speaks of the Eastern Shore Indians as "the best husbands

---
(1) Barlow's account in Hakluyt, iii, p.362.
(2) Cooke's Virginia, p.32.
(3) Waitz: Anthropologie iii, 31; Van Laet ii, 12; Smith, Generall Historie, bk.2, pp. 569,570.
(4) See "Brevis Narratio, etc." plate 22 of De Bry.
(5) See Cooke's, Burke's, Stith's, Campbell's Histories of Va.
(6) In Smith, Generall Hist. bk.4, pp.569,570.

(providers) of any Salvages we know"- Father White speaks of them, too, as "very tenacious of their purpose," and as being "possessed of a wonderful longing for civilized intercourse" with the English. He, moreover, goes on to describe them as frank, cheerful, quickwitted, possessing a keener sense of taste and smell than the English and what is more to their credit as "observing generous feeling toward all" and (as being) "full of gratitude for a favor shown them".

In intellectual and moral status, then, the Virginia Indian occupied a far higher scale than might have been expected from his general environment. Occupied, as he was, in satisfying his pressing wants by hunting, fishing or in agricultural pursuits, brief was the space he could devote to any mental cultivation: still in his narrow sphere of activity he was unsurpassed, and if barbarous, 'twas from his own willingness to be so, not from lack of capacity to become better.

In dress and attire the Virginia Indian was quite

---
(1) "Relatio Itineris etc." p.41; p.II of "Nova Britannia" in Force's Tracts, vol. 1.; Brown 1. p.265.
(2) "In universum maturunt liberales animos" vide "Relatio" p.41.
(3) Howe's Historical Collections of Va. p.138; Burke's History of Virginia iii, 49-82;

dainty in his own peculiar way, being passionately fond of trinkets. The upper part of his hair was commonly cut so as to form a ridge which stood up like the comb of a cock; while the hair of the right side of his head was shorn off; on the left side, it was worn at full length.(1) On the head were worn feathers of the wild-turkey, pheasant, hawk or other bird; in the ears, through which were pierced two or three "wyde holes, they hung fine shells with pearl drops, pieces of copper, "certaine fowles leggs" or "beasts claws".(2) Upon the breast were frequently worn(3) "Tablets of about four inches in diameter" polished very fine and made of fine smoothe shells, upon which was etched "birdes, stars, a Half-moon or any other figure suitable to the fancy"- Upon his neck and wrists hung strings of beads, peake or roenoke.(4) About the waist was an apron of deer-skin, gashed deeply about the edges, so that it appeared as it hung like tassels or fringe, and frequently at the upper edge of this fringe was an edging of peake.

Weapons such as the bow, arrow, targe, sword or battle axe were invariably carried, and quivers of fox-skin or

---
(1) Beverley, History of Va. pp. 128,129.
(2) Strachey, p.67.
(3) Beverley, Hist. of Va. pp. 180,181
(4) Shell - money. see Beverley: Hist. of Va. p.59. Intro

wolf-skin horribly adorned with the head or tail of the ani-
(1)
mal were in great estimation.   Common to all these Indians
(2)
also, certain "markings" on the shoulder-blades designating

the tribe to which each individual belonged and consequently

of a totemic significance.

Generally speaking, then, the clothing of the Vir-

ginia Indian consisted of the skins of beasts worn in winter
(3)
with the hair, in summer without.   "They are a people",
(4)
says Hariot in this connection, "clothed with loose mantles

made of deer-skin, and aprons of the same, made about the
(5)
middles, els all naked"; and in several accompanying plates

we are made acquainted with the costumes of the poorer and

richer classes; the priests, the conjurors, the elders, the

chiefs and the ladies are all represented to us in De Bry's
(5)
Plates. There were then, differences between the costumes of

the poorer and richer classes; for, while the latter fared

sumptuously "in large and flowing mantles of deer-skin," the

former had scarce to cover their nakedness but grass, leaves
(6)
of trees, etc.
----
(1) Howe's Historical Collections of Va. p.137; Beverley, p. 129.
(2) See Hariot's plate 22, entitled "The Markes of Sundrye of the Chiefe Men of Virginia."
(3) Archaeologia Americana IV,59; also Tables II.and III. in Beverley's Hist. of Va.
(4) Hariot in Hakuyt iii. 330.
(5) Plates IV,V,VI,VIII,IX,XII,XVI and XVIII.
(6) Smith in his Map of Va. p.66.

All females, as a usual thing, wore a semi-cuict of fur, being as Strachey says, very "shamefast to be seene bare"; but the "better sort" apparelled themselves in skin mantels, which were finely dressed, fringed and "carved". They also tatooed themselves in various real or fanciful designs, and frequently decorated themselves with beautifully woven mantels of turkey-feathers or silk-grass "exceedingly warm and handsome"- On the other hand, the younger women and children went nude until they were "nigh eleven or twelve returnes of the leafe olde", while both young and old went bare-foot, only a "priveleged few "enjoying the luxury of moccasins.

With regard to ornaments, copper beads and "paintings were most popular. The men painted their bodies black or yellow, and then, having anointed themselves with oil, they would stick in it the down of "sundry colored birds". When on the war-path, they would paint with streaks of bright red their foreheads, cheeks, and the right side of the head, the vermilion tint being brought about by the use of terra sigillata or the root pocone.

----

(1) Strachey, p.65.
(2) ibid
(3) Beverley Hist.of Va.p.132 and pl.vi. cf.Lawson: Hist. of Carolina, p.190.
(4) Strachey p.65. Beverly, Hist. of Va. p.128.
(5) Beverley, Hist. of Va. p.
(6) A common practice among barbarous peoples.cf Anc Britons
(7) Jones: Present State of Va. p.11.cf.Lawson,p.203;Brick-

(1)
It was a universal custom among the women to tatoo
their arms, breasts, thighs and shoulders in many fantastic
patterns, e.g., flowers, fruits snakes, etc. Cleanliness
was also a virtue limited to the females, but "conspicuous
for its absence" among the men. All paid great attention
to the arrangement of the hair: the married women wearing
it frequently a yard long on the left side of the head, but
shaving the other side, while the "mayds" always wore the
fore-part of the head and its sides shaven close and the
hinder part long." which they tie in a pleate hanging downe
to their hips." Their hair was always anointed with walnut
oil as a pomade, so that it was as sleek and glossy as a
raven's wing. Now and then, one especially desirous to
please would wear in the ear. "a small greene and yellow
colored snake scarce halfe a yard in length, which crawl-
inge and lapping herselfe about the necke often times fa-
(2)
miliarly would kiss his lips". Others of perhaps more
cultivated taste merely wore a "dead Rat tyed by the taile"
(3)
For head-gear some wore a sort of coronet some the wing of

the whole skin of a hawke, stuffed and with spread wings, others not to be outdone the "hand of their enemy dryed." [1]

Many different forms of adornment they used, says Smith, but he gives it as a general rule that "he is the most gallant, that is the most monstrous to behold." [2]

---

(1) Smith, Map of Va. p.66.
(2) ibid. 67; General Historie, bk. 2, p.36.

Chapter II.

DOMESTIC ECONOMY, ~~HP~~ ~~ANI~~ ~~OCCUPATIONS~~

The habitations of the Virginia Indians were either oven-like in shape or else oblong with a curved roof. They were built "commonly upon a rice of a hill" by the river-side or near some fresh spring. These wigwams, for so we may call them, were most usually constructed by bending
(1)
small saplings, tying them, and closely thatching the frame-work with "matts throne over" or the "barkes of trees" leaving two openings for doors "one before and a
(2)
posterne"; so that when complete they appeared like "little garden arbours." So well were such rude structures adapted to their use, that in all weathers they were comparatively comfortable and protective, though in winter they were of course quite dark and smoky, for the fire being built in the centre of the habitation, the smoke had to pervade the whole dwelling before making its exit through
(3)
an aperture in the apex of the roof. Nor was the wigwam

the Virginia-Indian. They, like the Iroquois of New York, had also that peculiar form of structure known as the "Long
(1)
House". These as known to the "Ancient Virginians" were from twelve to twenty-four yards in length by from six to
(2)
ten yards in breadth; and their existence implies the existence of a sort of communal life among them.

Their beds consisted of little bundles of reeds covered with a "fyne white matte or twoo" elevated about a foot from the ground by means of a "hurdle" of wood. These were invariably placed right against the fire. The Indians in sleeping, invariably reclined "heads by points" one by one with their feet to the fire, some covered with skins or mats and others stark naked "as doe the Irish" remarks
(3)
Strachey en passant. As many as twenty would frequently dwell in the same "house" and same room. Their only utensils were baskets of silk-grass, gourds, or earthern pots,
(4)
fragments of which still cover the spots once occupied by such Indian dwellings; and their sites are still to be identified by deposits of oyster and muscle shells found in

The Virginia Indians had various "towns", but the largest of them contained not more than twenty or thirty "houses", standing "dissite and scattered without forme of a street, far and wyde assunder":[1] the population of such towns ranged from fifty to five hundred, several families usually inhabiting one house which was quite large, as has been intimated above.

Sometimes fortified in a rude manner, these towns were for the most part open and defenceless. We have plates illustrating both kinds;[2] the fortified in plate XIX[3] of the ""Admiranda Narratio," the unfortified in the "Brevis Narratio" plate XX representing the town of Secota. In this plate are to be seen fields of tobacco and maize in the vicinity of the village, and the relative positions of their places of prayer, feasting, dancing, idol-worship, reservoirs or places of getting water,[4] fire-temples and the mausoleum of their kings. One or more of such towns constituted in the view of the old chroniclers a "Kingdom".

In their domestic relations and family structure, it will be enough to state that the family-type of the Virginia Indians was, to use the nomenclature of Mr. L. H. Morgan,[1] the syndyasmian or pairing. Instead of the large groups presented by lower types of sexual union, the Virginia Indians had definitely organised married pairs, and so a clearly marked family-structure. It is to be distinctly added, however, that communism of wives (i.e., the communal family-type) was by no means unknown: indeed it is indicated by the cohabitation of families in one "long house." A proof of such a communal family-type having existed in Virginia is given by the prevalence through all the tribes without exception of the practice of reckoning kinship through females.[2] This sort of kinship it is generally agreed, is the natural product and result of promiscuous intercourse between the sexes; for, when a child was born, the mother of course being known, and the father unknown, the logical consequence was that the child having no father had relatives only in its mother and her kinsmen.[3]

---
(1) Morgan: Ancient Society, pp. 384,453 and following.
(2) See Hariot, Smith, Strachey, Hakluyt's Voyages, Beverly et alii.
(3) See Morgan's Ancient Society C.6.; Jones' Antiquities of the Southern Indians, p.23; Lawson, p.195. Cf.Heroditus, 1, 173; Odyssey, 1, 206.

Courtship was short, simple and unembarassing in character. If the presents of the young warrior were accepted by the parents of his intended bride, and he gave them proof that he was capable of properly supporting a wife, she was considered as having become his spouse: (1) This — a beautiful custom among all North American tribes - is charmingly illustrated by Longfellow in his description of Hiawatha's courtship. Marriage took place invariably at an early age; females about fourteen, males at about eighteen years old, becoming paired. In most respects it stood upon the same footing among the Virginia Indians as among the other North American tribes. That is to say it was based on convenience, negotiated without the knowledge or acquiescence of the contracting parties and solemnized by no priestly intervention: still, for the most part, the marriage tie was held sacred and inviolable, and contracted with much ceremony. (2) Such a marriage-ceremony is described by Henry Spelman (3) as follows: "The parents bringes ther daughter betwene them (if her parents be deade, then some of her kinsfolke, or whom it pleaseth the king to apoynt

---
(1) Strachey, p.109. cf. Hawkins' Sketch of the Creek Confederacy; Jefferson's Notes, pp. 340-342.
(3) Spelman: Relation of Virginia, p. cvii.

(for ye man goes not unto any place to be married but ye woman is brought to him where he dwelleth). At her cominge to him, her father or chiefe friends ioynes ye hands togither the father or chiefe friend of ye man bringeth a longe stringe of beades, and measuringe his armes leangth thereof doth breake it over ye heads of thos that are to be maried while ther hands be ioyned togither and gives into ye womans father or to him that brings her and so with much mirth and feastinge they goe together."

Though Spelman's account would seem to imply monogamy as existing among the Virginia Indians, polygamy was frequent (1) and was practised by all who could afford it; but as a "multiplicitie of women" was a expensive luxury, it was only the "better sort" who could afford it: so that most of these Indians had to be content with one wife. (2)

As a general rule, the Virginia Indian never married a member of his own tribe. "In their marriages", Pory tells us, "they observe a large distance, as well in affinitie as consanguinitie." The marriage tie continued only during the pleasure of the parties; the husband could put away his wife at pleasure, and the wife had a like privi-

----
(1) "Plures ducunt uxores" says Father White, "integram tamen servant conjugulem fidem"- Arch.Amer. IV, 64.
(2) Strachey, p.114; cf. Lawson's History of Carolina, p. 187.
(3) See Smith's Generall Historie, bk.4. p.570.

(1)
lege. The continuance of the marriage-relation, then, varied at the option of the parties, still there was a public sentiment against divorce, and reconciliation was always attempted between dissatisfied parties.(2)

In married life the women were required to be chaste and infidelity was unpardonable; still, however, with the husband's assent, the wife would readily yield to the advances of an admirer.(3) As for the unmarried Indian maidens, they were generally chaste,(4) for if they had "a child when they are single, it is such a disgrace that they can never get husbands": on the other hand, it is to be noted, that the men were by no means of such good character they were extremely licentious,(5) and we are told that the "great disease" was prevalent among them.(6)

Both husband and wife, in their married life, had well-defined duties;(7) his it was to hunt, fish, go on the war-path, attend the councils of his tribe, build the boat or fell the tree: hers, to prepare the food, watch the children, carry the burdens, plant, weed and grind the corn,(8) make

---
(1) Howe's Historical Collections of Va. p.140; Jones' Antiquities of the Southern Indians, p.66
(2) Morgan's Ancient Society, pp.159-185. cf. Jones' Antiquities of the Southern Indians, pp. 65-69.
(3) Strachey, p.110
(4) Beverley, Hist.of Va. p.127; Byrd's Westover Mss.
(5) Strachey, p.110

the basket and pottery, and finally perform the office of
barber to their husbands.(1) Hers was, indeed the laboring
one, and well might the Indian husband say of his wife as
Petruchio said of Catherine:(2)

> "She is my goods and chattels; she is my house,
> My household stuff, my field, my barn,
> My horse, my ox, my ass, my anything."

The wife, however, was by no means, without privileges. Marriage gave the husband no right over the property of the wife; the husband occupied the position of a man visitor in his wife's house; and, in case of separation, merely took up his bundle and departed; nor did this separation entail any disgrace on either party to the transaction.(3) In marriage relations, further, it should be noted, that traces of an older stage of promiscuity still existed; for, it would seem from numerous hints(4) thrown out by various authors that in some cases no exclusive cohabitation existed among the Virginia tribes, but the women dispensed their favors among a certain circle of males; a state of

---
(1) Smith's Map of Va. p.67; Howe, p.141; Gen. Hist. bk.2 p.361.
(2) Shakespeare's "Taming of the Shrew".
(3) Howe, p.140; Morgan, Anc't Soc. p.454; Jones, Antiq. of So. Indians, p.66.
(4) Strachey, pp. 53-54; Spelman, p. c.viii.

affairs indicated by the communal life of the "Long House."[1] However this may be, on the separation of a married couple, the children belonged to the mother not to the father;[2] though Beverly informs us that in some cases, they were equally divided.

That a high respect and esteem was entertained for the Indian ladies of Virginia is evidenced by their custom of having female chiefs or sachems who had often great weight in the tribal councils.[3] Another curious custom goes to prove the fact still further, illustrating as it does some delicacy of feeling; that is to say, the custom of keeping pregnant women in a sort of "gynaeceum" apart from the men,"nor will they at such time press into the nursery where they are," avers Strachey.[4]

Of the domestic life of these Indians we have some few notices. Henry Spelman[5] speaks of their "Setting at Meate" as follows: "They sett on matts round about the house, the men by themselves, the weomen by themselves. The weomen bring to everyone a dish of meate for the better

---
(1) See Supra. pp.31,32.
(2) C.C.Jones, p.56; Beverly, p.134; Burke,iii, 61,62.
(3) Cf. Smith's "Queen of Appomatuck" and Queene of Paspategh", Beverly's "Empress of Pandye"
(4) Strachey, p.68.
(5) Spelman's Relation of Virginia, p. cxiii.

sort never eat together in one dish. When he hath eaten
what he will, or that which was given him, for he looks for
no second corse, he setts downe his dish by and mumbleth
certayne words to himselfe in manner of (a saying grace)
givinge thanks, if any be leaft the weomen gather it up and
either keep it till the next meall or gives it to the poorer sort if any be ther"-

Rather more explicit statements with regard to et-
iquette at meals are given us by Beverley.(1) He tells us
that the Virginia Indian's fashion of setting at meals was
upon a mat spread on the ground, with the dish between
their legs, which were extended at full length before them;
and it was only very rarely that more than two sat together
at one dish, presumably both because of their enormous ap-
petite, and too,for the very good reason that more than two
could not "conveniently mix their legs together and have
the dish stand commodiously for both".(2)

The chief eating utensil was the spoon, and this we
are told usually held half a pint or more; and with regard
to its use they would laugh at the English for using small
ones "which they must be forced to carry so often to their
mouths that their arms are in danger of being tired before

---
(1) Beverley, Hist. of Va. p.141. He also gives a plate
    showing "An Indian and his wife at Dinner"-
(2) ibid. p.141.

their belly."- "Old Virginia 'hospitality was found then as now, and very quaint and entertaining are the numerous accounts of Indian feasts and dances in honor of their guests given by the early travellers in those regions.(1)

The women, we are told, were easily delivered of child and loved their offspring very dearly. As soon as a child was born, it was dipped "head over ears" in cold water, and then bound to a board prepared for such a function. The infant was kept so fastened and bound to the board till able to crawl, being released therefrom on a few occasions only.(2) To make their young children hardy which, as at Sparta, was the main end of "education" in Virginia, they were washed in the snow in the coldest mornings;(3) and by paint and "oyntments" their skins were so tanned and toughened that after a year or two no weather could hurt them.(4)

(1) When a child was named, the neighbors and kinsfolk (i.e., gentiles) were invited to the cabin of the parents.

Before this assemblage the father took the child in

---

(1) See account in Beverley, Archer, Strachey, Smith, Hakluyt, Harris and others.
(2) Beverley. Hist. of Va. pp.134,135; see also Mode of Carrying Children in Virginia plate opp. p.134
(3) Smith's Generall Historie. bk.3,p.363; Map of Va.p.67
(4) Smith, Map of Va. p.67.
(5) Spelman: Relation of Virginia, p.   c ix.

his arms and gave it a name, which it retained through life, after which solemnity the day was spent in song and the dance.(1) In order to render their children expert in that chief source of support to the American Indian - archery - the mothers would deprive their boys of food, till they could hit a mark set up for them to shoot at; and such was the degree of skill to which they could attain by such a discipline that they could easily hit small objects at an almost incredible distance. To hurl the tomahawk, dance the war-dance and cast the spear were also fundamental parts of their "education".(2) "In youth", says Strachey,(3) "the children are given some affectionate title, but when they become able to travel in the woods, and go forth hunting and fishing, the father gives another name as he finds him apt and of spirit to prove brave and valiant." And from such a practice, which existed, as we know, both among males and females it is highly probable that a confusion

highly probable that he had several of them. The Pocahontas (aged 10) who saved Smith in May, 1608;[1] the Pocahontas alias Amonate[2] who, Strachey says, was "married to a private captain called Kocoum in 1610; and the Pocahontas alias Matoaka[3] (aged 18) who married Rolfe in 1614 imply at least two different persons. Hence, it may reasonably be assumed that the lovely character who saved Smith and the colony of Virginia and was honorably married to Rolfe in 1613 (Matoax* is not to be confounded with the wanton scape-grace - Amonate * who was married to "Captain Kocoum" in 1610, and who was in the habit of playing the tomboy at the English fort. For Pocahontas is mentioned by Strachey as being an "affectionate title" or nick-name given to her as the pet of the family just as we should use some such expression as "little tomboy" or little "rascal". We are then, assuredly justified in making the assumption (in as much as the Indians in general had but two names: a real and a nick-name) that the old "Emperour" might have

---
(1) Smith in Newes from Virginia"
(2) Strachey says "When they are young, their mother gives them some affectionate title (nick-name) and so the great King Powhatan called a young daughter of his Pocahontas, which may signify "little wanton': howbeit she was more rightly called Amonate at more ripe years."
(3) According to Stith, pp. 136,285 this was her real name
(4) Powhatan, it would seem, had three names, viz. Powhatan, Wahunsecawh and Ottaniock. But "Wahunsecawh" was the name "by which he was saluted (Strachey, p.48) consequently it was a title of honor, while Powhatan was a local not a personal name: so that when called the "Emperour of Virginia", Pow-

had two separate and distinct little pets or wantons in his numerous and constantly growing family, whose real names were respectively in their later years Amonate and Matoax. Such an assumption is still further warranted by a descrepancy in the ages of the "Pocahontases" above mentioned, and is still further strengthened when we learn that the real name of a Virginia Indian was rarely uttered, as it was believed among them that a knowledge of the real names of persons gave their enemies power to cast spells over them.(1)

The food of the Virginia Indians was largely obtained by hunting and fishing. Naturally, then, they took their chief pride and pleasure in such sports, and an additional incentive to activity and courage in such pursuits was the fact that by such qualities they gained their wives, who (sensible girls!) were not so much attracted by men's address and gallantry as by the expectation of plenty of food; for, as Strachey(2) informs us in his pedantic way, "they be all of them large eaters and of whom we save with
----
hatan much as we would call the Emperor of Russia "Runa". The inference would be, then, that his real name was Ottaniack.
(1) Cooke (History of Va. p.103) following Stith (Hist. of Va. pp.136,285), says "Pocahontas . . . . was her household name, and she was Powhatan's dearest daughter"- He, however, like the other Virginia historians confuses Pocahontas Amonate with Pocahontas Matoax.
(2) Strachey, pp. 75,77.

Plautus "noctes diesque estur"- From their activity in this way, they of course became acquainted with all the places most frequented by game of all sorts.

It was a custom of theirs to go on a hunting expedition [1] into "the deserts" some three or four days journey in parties of two to three hundred together, "almost as the Tartars doe" says Strachey, carrying with them their hunting houses and women "with corne, acorns, mortars and all bag and baggage they use"- When such a hunting party found the deer, they surrounded them with many fires, between which they placed themselves, while some took up a position in the centre. The deer frightened by such unaccustomed noise and lights would become stampeded, running round and round in a circle. In such a condition of fright as many as six, eight, ten or even fifteen were killed at a hunting by their adroit use of the bow and arrow [2] in the hands of the Indian archers.

Again, they sometimes drove the deer into a narrow point of land, and then into the water, where they could be easily killed as they swam by men in boats.

----
(1) Smith's Generall Historie, bk.2, pp. 365,366.
(2) See Percy in Brown's Genesis of the United States,1, 162; Smith's Generall Historie, bk.2, p.365; Purchas His Pilgrimes IV, 1685.

(1)
Just as the Bushmen of South Africa used, in stalking the ostrich use ostrich's feathers, skin, etc., so did the Virginia Indian in stalking the deer alone disguise himself in a deer-skin slit on one side, and so put his arm through the neck that his hand came to the head that was stuffed, and the horns, head, eyes, ears and every part was as artificially counterfeited as possible - (2) Thus disguised with stealthy step he would come upon the deer, creeping along the ground from one tree to another till he could get a fair shot; then, having wounded it, he could chase the exhausted animal till he overtook it.

Fishing was done principally in boats called quintans (3), with hand-nets, woven with bark of certain trees and deer-sinews. Angles, too, were frequently used: these were small rods with the end cleft, in which a line was fastened, and to this line a hook deftly made of bone was attached. Long arrows (i.e., harpoons) with a line attached were employed for spearing fish in the rivers; (4) the Accomac Indians using bone-headed javelins for this purpose. (5)

Ingeniously-made weirs were also common. In plate xiii of the "Admiranda Narratio", we find a distinct repre-
----
(1) Cf. Livingstone's Travels.
(2) Smith's Generall Historie, bk.2, pp. 365,366.
(3) See Plate 36 of the "Brevis Narratio".
(4) See plate xiii of the "Admiranda Narratio".
(5) See Smith, Generall Historie, bk.2, p.365.

sentation of one of these fish-traps with extended wings; one of which reaches to the shore, and the other far out into the water. It is made of canes or small poles firmly stuck in the mud, so as to preserve an upright position. Placed closely together, and rising a few feet above the water-level, they are securely fastened together by parallel ropes or withes, basket-fashion, and so form a sort of fence through which the fish are unable to pass. In the centre is an opening leading into a circular enclosure: this by a circuitous opening communicates with a second pen, and this in like manner with a third, and that, in its turn with a fourth; each somewhat smaller than the former. Two Indians are to be seen in a canoe at the opening of the weir, one with a net dipping up the fish thus entangled and bewildered.

The Virginia Indians divided the year into five seasons. The winter they called Popanow; spring, Cattapeak; summer, Cohattagough; the earing of the corn, Nepinough; harvest and the fall of the leaf, Taquitock. They, however reckoned the years by winters or cohonks as they were called. This is an onomatopoeic word indicating so many passages of the wild-geese from north to south, i.e., so many

----
(1) See Smith, Generall Historie, bk. 2, p.357; Strachey, p.29; Howe, p.139; Beverley, p.56.

(1)
winters.

The years were also reckoned by moons, though not with any relation to so many in a year as we are used to doing; but the moons recurred with them at regular times and with a regular name, c.e., "moon of stags", the "sorn-moon", and the first and second "moon of cohonks". There was no distinction with them of the hours of the day; though, on the other hand, they divided it into three parts; the rise, the power, and the lowering of the sun; and they kept their accounts or what not by knotted strings like the
(2)
Peruvian quippas.   From September to the middle of November
(3)
ber were their chief feasts and sacrifices.

been previously cleared and cleansed of weeds. Large portions of Virginia, then, before the arrival of the whites were far from being uncultivated, and the following beautiful description of an Indian village by Longfellow[2] would apply equally well to scores of picturesque villages with their "cone-like cabins" in Virginia:-

> "All around the happy village
> Stood the maize-fields, green and shining
> Waved the green plumes of Mondanim,
> Waved his soft and sunny tresses,
> Filling all the land with plenty."

By far the most laborious part of Indian agriculture was, as might be expected, the preparation of the ground for planting by the removal of the primeval forest. This was effected by bruising the trees near the roots, which were then scorched with fire and grubbed to prevent further growth. When by this means the trees were burnt nearly through, they were uprooted and pushed over with the aid of stone-axes.[3] The following year both men and women with crooked pieces of wood "in forme of mattocks or hoes with long handles" went around the fields beating up the "weeds,

---
(1) Strachey, 60, 72, 117.
(2) Hiawatha.
(3) See plate in Beverley p. 183; Smith, Gen.Hist. bk.2, p.364; Strachey, P.68 and Spelman's "Relation.

grass, and old stubble" by the roots. In ground thus laboriously prepared, the corn was planted almost exactly as we plant it to this day. A hole was first made in the ground with a pointed stick and into each hole four grains of corn and two beans were placed and duly covered up. In fields thus planted with "hills of corn" about four feet apart men, women and children were kept constantly busy weeding till the corn-stalk had attained half its proper height.(1)

In plate xxi of the "Brevis Narratio" six Indians are to be seen busily at work preparing the ground and planting corn. No fence or enclosed space of any kind are represented. From the explanatory note it would appear that the Virginia Indians diligently cultivated the soil, using for the purpose fish-bones attached to wooden handles. By means of such rude agricultural implements, these Indians broke up and made even the surface of the ground. Following after the men come the women who, with sticks, made holes in the ground just prepared. Into these holes beans and grains of corn were dropped. In planting their corn, then, the Virginia Indians exercised a great degree of care, but their energy ended here, for, after having ac-
----
(1) Hariot's account in Hakluyt iii, 329; C.C. Jones' Antiquities of the Southern Indians, pp.41, 307.

complished this, the corn was for the most part left to
take care of itself. Most of this agricultural work devolved upon the women, who both planted and harvested the crop
but they were greatly assisted by a servile class of men
(1)
and the better-grown children. The corn when gathered was
stored away in the store-house of the village, and kept under the charge of the chief-man.
(2)

When the corn, planted as above described, had grown
up, the beans which had been planted therewith, of course
grew up as well, running up the corn-stalks like "hops on
poles" as Spelman expresses it. From the same authority
(3)
we learn the Indian methods of gathering, harvesting, shelling and grinding the corn; and these differ in so slight
a degree from present methods that it will be superfluous
to give them in detail.

The planting of corn took place in April, but chiefly in May and was continued till the middle of June. What
was planted respectively in April, May and June, was reaped
in August, September and October. The variety of corn
(4)
cultivated by the Virginia Indians to such a wide extent

----
(1) See plate xxiii of the "Brevis Narratio"; infra, p.93
(2) See plate xxii of the "Brevis Narratio"; also Smith's
    Generall Historie, bk.   p.
(3) Spelman's Relation of Virginia, p.cxi.
(4) Smith's Generall History, bk.2, p.358.

bore two to four ears to a stalk and upon each ear were about two to three hundred grains. Peas and beans were likewise widely cultivated by these "Ancient Virginians" as well as all sorts of melons and fruits; (1) and, we are also informed that turkies were tamed by them in large droves.
(2)
Smith describes the way the Virginia Indians had of preparing corn, as follows: "Their corne they rost in the eare green, and bruising it in a mortar of wood with a Polt, lapp it into rowles in the leaves of their corne, and so boyle it for a daintie. They also reserve that corne late planted that will not ripe, by roasting it in hot ashes, the heat thereof drying it. In winter they esteeme it being boyled with beanes a rare dish they call Pawscorow-mena. The old wheat they first steepe a night in hot water, in the morning pounding it in a morter. They use a small basket for their temmes, then pound againe the great, and so, separating by dashing their hand in the basket, receive the flower in a platter made of wood, scraped to that forme with burning it and shels. Tempering this flower with water, they make it either in cakes, covering them in ashes till they be baked and then washing them in faire wa-
----
(1) ibid. p.359 and infra. p.55
(2) Smith's Gen. Hist. Bk.2, p.356; Percy in Purchas, IV. 1685-1690.

ter, they drie presently with their owne heat or else boyle them in water eating the broth with the bread which they call 'Ponap'.

Cookery

[handwritten marginal notes, largely illegible]

lished cooks, ture a "cook-rn for food what is h-cake - that urvives in would seem endant of the (2) iny" or space water over a other dish of cooking l". This was ich the meat as either impaled on the end of one stick fastened in the ground or else laid upon several sticks gridiron-fashion, raised upon forked sticks two feet or more above the live coals. This mode of cooking has the advantage of heating

---
(1) "Victitant plerumque pulte quam Pone et omini appel-
and   ant; utremque ex tritico(indico)conficitur adduntque
(2)   interdum prolem, vel quod venatu, ancepio quo associ-
       tique sunt.
(3)   See Table IV. of Beverley, p.139.

ter, then drie presently with their owne heat or else boyle them in water eating the broth with the bread which they call 'Ponap'"-

The Virginia Indians were, then, accomplished cooks, living witnesses to the fact that man is by nature a "cooking animal." The favorite way of preparing corn for food among the Virginia Indians, then, is evidently what is known among modern Virginians as baking the ash-cake - that well-known delicacy, and their "ponap" still survives in the corn-pone of the Virginia darkies; for, it would seem that this word "pone" is etymologically a descendant of the Indian "ponap"(1), not the Latin "paris"(2). "Hominy" or cracked up Indian corn, soaked, husked and boiled in water over a gentle fire from two to twelve hours, is yet another dish originating among these Indians; and our mode of cooking called "barbecuing"(3) is yet another "survival". This was one of their modes of broiling- the one in which the meat was either impaled on the end of one stick fastened in the ground or else laid upon several sticks gridiron-fashion, raised upon forked sticks two feet or more above the live coals. This mode of cooking has the advantage of heating

----
(1) and (2) "Victitant plerumque pulte quam Pone et omini appelant; utremque ex tritico(indico)conficitur adduntque interdum prolen, vel quod venatu, ancepio que assecutique sunt.
(3) See Table IV. of Beverley, p.139.

gradually, and at the same time dries up all extra mois-
(1)
ture.

In preparing the meats of wild animals, these were all skinned and gutted, and the fowls picked; but fish were dressed with the scales and ungutted. Excellent broth was made by them out of the "head and umbles" of the deer, which "all bloody were put into the pot" this decoction Beverley likens to the famous black broth (————) of (2)   (3)
the ancient Lacaedamonians. Indian corn gathered while young and milky and roasted before the fire - "roasting-ears"- was considered a great delicacy, and besides eating their corn in this way the Virginia Indians had two other modes of preparing corn: viz. (1) Ustatahomen, made of groats and the coarser pieces of corn (after fanning away the lighter portions) boiled together in water three or four hours. (2) Pohytough, a mixture of corn-meal and
(4)
burnt corn-cob.

The Virginia Indians, indeed, had a great variety of food both in the natural products of the earth, fish, flesh and fowl, and also in the fruits of their agricultural labors. They lived on all sorts of birds, for "of them they

---
(1) Beverley, p.138; Parlowe's account in Hakluyt, iii.30
(2) Beverley, p.139.
(3) The "Pagatour" of Hariot, iii, pp.320,329.
(4) Spelman, p.cvi.   Smith's Gen.Hist. bk.2,pp.352-357; Strachey, pp. 114-130; Beverley, pp. 137-141.

had "great store only peacocks and common hens wanting. Almost every variety of wild animal supplied them with meat; deer, "goates", squirrels, "stages", aronghcun, assapanick, (squirrils) musascus (musk-rat), bears, beavers, otters, foxes, opossums, hares, etc., were abundant. Fish of all kinds teemed in the rivers, bays and creeks. "Sodden wheate", peas, beans and pulse were always eaten, and when these were not at hand the Indians did not disdain as articles of food grubs, the nymphae of wasps, scarabaei, cicadae and such like articles. Bread was made not only of corn, as we have noticed, but also of wild-oats and the seeds of the sun-flower. For a relish, the ashes of hickory, stickweed, or some other such plant was, as they appear to have had no salt. In their "gardens" near the towns cherries, peaches, strawberries, grapes, cushaws, melons, pumpkins, plums and persimmons were cultivated with care; and these fruits were not only eaten but dried and preserved.

Chinquapins, chestnuts, hickories and walnuts were highly esteemed, but hazle-nuts appear to have been little esteemed by these curious people. The kernels of such nuts beaten in a mortar with water added would form a thick milky fluid; this they called Pawcohiccora and greatly was

---
(1) Strachey, p.115

it esteemed. Acorns were made into bread, or else oil was extracted from them. Earth-nuts, cuttanimmons, rawcomens wild-onions and tuckahoe root "of a very hot and virulent quality" (of which a sort of bread was made) were also important articles of food.

Another of the great staples of ancient Virginia was tobacco. Strachey, (1) however, assures us that it was "not of the best Kynd", and then proceeds to describe the way in which it was used: among them ...... the Salvages here dry the leaves of the apocke (2) over the fier, and sometymes in the sun, and pmtable yt into poulder, stalks leaves and all, taking the same in pipes of earth which very ingeniously they make".

Subsisting, then as they did, mainly upon the generosity of nature and chiefly by hunting and fishing, the Virginia Indians were under the necessity of changing their diet as the seasons changed. (3) In March and April they lived chiefly upon animal food and their fishing weirs, feeding on fish, turkies or squirrels; in May and June they planted their fields and lived principally on the spontaneous products of the earth or water -acorns, walnuts and

eat, it was a common usage among them to disperse in small companies and live thus separated upon strawberries, mulberries, terrapins, oysters, crabs or fish or green corn. As a result of and at the same time as evidence of their utter dependance upon nature's bounty, we are informed by Captain Smith (1) that, like the wild-beasts their bodies altered with their diet and were fat or lean according to the season of the year. How great soever their variety of food their only drink, says Strachey, (2) was "cliere water"; this they drank "as the Turkes doe: for albeit they have grapes, and thereof good store, yet they have not value upon the use of them nor advised to presse them into wyne". It was not till the arrival of the civilized white-men that "aquavitae" was enticed from the grains of their Pagatour.

------

(1) Smith's Generall Historie, bk. 2, p.363; Map of Va. p.69
(2) Strachey, p.63. Beverley (p.141) tells us that their preference was for pond-water heated by the rays of the sun.

Chapter III.
COMMERCE, HANDICRAFTS, DIVERSIONS, WRITING, MEDICINE.

Of course the arrival of the English colonists and their active intercourse with the various Indian tribes of Virginia stimulated their trading instincts,[1] and caused them very soon to put a true valuation upon their rude wealth[2] with reference to articles of English manufacture. Still, however, there must have been quite an active commerce and trade going on among the different tribes before the arrival of the whites. The existence of such a widespread system of inter-tribal barter is frequently alluded to by contemporary writers. Smith,[3] for instance, (and in this he is corroborated by others) mentions the fact of having seen Indians in Virginia with copper ornaments and tools which must have come from the copper mines of Lake Superior or other far distant regions. The same writer tells us of people dwelling in certain localities in Virginia whom he characterizes as the "best merchants of all other Savages." Though most of their transactions were by barter, money in a crude sense at least existed among them;

---
(1) Beverley. p.195; Byrd, Westover Mss. 1, p.180.
(2) See "Report of Fr. Magnel" in Brown's "Genesis" 1. p.136
(3) Smith: Generall Hist. bk.3, p.415 and bk. 2, pp.350,351 Map of Va. p. 74; Howe, p.138.

peake, roanoke and copper playing the part of media of exchange. Pipes, runtees and pearls are also to be noted as varieties of the "Treasure" and "Riches" of the Indian of Virginia.

Discoidal stones, pipes, beautifully fashioned, spear-and arrow-points and other articles manufactured exclusively by the Indians of the inland countries and mountainous districts were readily exchanged by a class of intermediaries (= "marchants") with the coast-tribes who gave in return therefore shells, pearls and commodities peculiar to their part of the country, and consequently of value to

---
(1) "Peak" says Beverley (p. 180), "is of two sorts or rather colors, for both are made of one shell though of different parts; one is a dark purple cylinder, and the other a white. They are both made in size and figure alike and commonly much resembling the English Buglas, but not so transparent nor so brittle. They are strung by a hole drilled through the centre. The dark purple is the dearest and is distinguished by the name of Wampum peak. The Indian traders value the Wampum peak at eighteen pence per yard and the white peak at nine pence." cf. Lawson's Hist. of Carolina, p. 315; Brickell, p. 327 et seq.
(2) Roanoke was "made of the Cockle shell, broke into small bits with rough edges, drilled through in the same manner as beads. It was used as the Peak. see Beverley, p.180.
(3) Jones' Antiquities of the So. Indians. p.502.
(4) Pipes were made of Peak, two or three inches long and thicker than ordinary: Beverley, p. 181

the hill people. Proof positive of such commercial relations exists in the fact that the shell-heaps and relic beds of Eastern Virginia contain, as we shall see below, various articles of utility or ornament brought from a distance; and, it is a particularly fact that the very finest specimens are thus obtained at the furthest distances from the spot whence the material used in their manufacture was procured.(1)

Great skill and persevering ingenuity is evidenced by the manufacture and preparation of such shell-money, wampum-peak and other articles of ornamentation among the Virginia Indians, nor were their energies directed solely in this direction, for their proficiency in the manufacture of weapons and household utensils, in pottery, weaving and a rude metallurgy was almost equally marked. The skill in "handicrafts"(2), indeed, exhibited by these Virginia Indians was far from contemptible, nor was their artistic skill by any means mediocre for barbarians as they were.(3) "In their

---
(1) See Jones' Antiquities of the Southern Indians, pp.63, 64 and cf. Rau's "Tauschverhältnisse der Eingebornen Nord Amerikas" in Archiv für Anthropologie.
(2) See Peverley, pp. 182,183; Smith: Gen. Hist. bk.2,pp. 364,365; Strachey, p.68.
(3) The Virginia Indians were in the Lower or Middle Status of Barbarism according to Mr. L.H.Morgan's classification. See his Ancient Society. p.152.

proper manner", says Hariot, "they seeme very ingenious . . . . .show excellencie of wit." The direction of such ingenuity and "excellencie of wit" was naturally, mainly in the manufacture of weapons or implements of utility in war or the chase.

Bows were made into the proper form by scraping down staves of locust or hiccory to the proper thickness by aid of a shell; arrows were fashioned of straight sprigs or reeds and headed with bone, flint, crystal, or even the spur of the wild-turkey or beak of some bird; they were "fledged" with turkey-feathers. Their shields were round and made of the bark of certain trees and silk-grass, and so compactly were they woven that they were impenetrable by an arrow. Their swords were fashioned of hiccory wood, very large and "like such wooden instruments as our English women swingle their flax withal." Instead of a sword, use was frequently made of a sort of rude battle-axe made of the bone of a deer put through a piece of wood like a pick-axe or hoe. A splinter of reed or shell served as

----
(1) In Hakluyt iii, 336; in Howk's Hist. of North Carolina 1, p.180.
(2) Beverley, p. 182; Strachey, p. 105; Smith, Gen: Hist. bk. 2, p. 364; Hakluyt's Voyages iii. 332.
(3) Indian targets, says Smith, (Gen. Hist. bk. iii. p.425) were "made of little small sticks woven betwixt strings of hempe and silk-grass, as is our cloth --no arrow can penetrate them."
(4) Strachey, p.68; De Bry's "Brevis' Narrato" plate iii.

a knife, and a bear's tooth "notched" their arrows; arrow-points were attached to the shaft of the arrow by a glue made of sinews. Boats, quintans or canoes "like the auncyent monoxylum navigium" were fashioned out of the trunk of a single tree. (1) The tree was first felled by means of fire and stone-axes, then a fire was built upon its trunk as it lay upon the ground, and the burnt and scorched parts scraped away with stones and shells until it at length assumed the shape of a trough; some of these "quintans" were as much as three feet deep and forty feet long and would accommodate as many as thirty men. (2) They were propelled not by oars but by paddles or sticks; and with

---

(1) Trees were felled by fire not by tools, see plate opp. p. 183 of Beverley.

(2) De Bry in his "Admiranda Narratio" pl.xii describes the manufacture of canoes by the Va. Indians as follows: "Mira est in Virginia cymbas fabricandi ratio; nam cum ferreis instrumentis aut aliis nostris similibus careant, eas tamen parare norunt nostris non minus commodas ad navigan-vum quo lubet per flumina et ad piscandum. Primum arbore aliqua crassa et alta dilecta, pro cymbae quam parare volunt magnitudine, ignem circa eius radices summa tellure in ambitu struunt ex arborore musco bene resiccato et lignisulis paulatim ignem excitantes, ne flamma altius ascendat ot arboris longitudinem minuat. Paene adusta et ruinam minante arbore, novum suscitant ignem quem flagrare sinunt donec arbor sponte cadat. Adustis deinde arboris fastigio et ramis et truncas instam longitudinem retineat tignis, transversis supra furcas positis imponunt erea altitudine ut commode laborare possint tunc cortice conchis quibusdam ademto integrioram trunci partem pro cymbae inferiore parte servant in altera parte ignem secundun trunci longitudinem struunt praeterquam extremis quod satis addustum illis videtur restricto igne cochis scabunt et novo suscitato igne, denuo addurunt itta deinceps pergunt subind urentes et scabentes donec symba necessarium alvum nucte sit.

such rude means of propulsion as these assisted by their
hands and feet, they would fly through the water with in-
(1)
credible speed.

Of shells of various species (clam, cockle, land-
tortoise, oyster, mussel, conch, etc.) the Virginia Indians
(2)
manufactured for themselves eating utensils, spoons,
(3)   (4)   (5)
drinking-cups   knives,   tweezers,   rattles, gougers,
(6)
chisels, scrapers etc.; in fact, shells were in common use
as weapons for war or the chase, for agricultural implements, fishing and in a variety of arts (e.g. pottery).

Varieties of shells, also were material out of which
beads, bead-ornaments, etc. were made; and, as is well
known, shells as wampum-peake (sc. money) played an exceed-
(7)
ingly important part in Indian economy. From salt-water
and lacustrine shells, too, were obtained pearls; these
were perforated, strung and worn around the neck, arms,
wrists, waist and ankles. Other articles of adornment made

---
(1) Smith, Gen. Hist. bk.2, p.364. Bark canoes were sel-
    dom seen in Virginia.
(2) Beverley, (p.154) speaks of a "cockle-shell . they
    sometimes used insteadof a spoon."
(3) See "Brevis Narrato" plate xxix.
(4) Beverley (p.97) speaks of "Knives . . . of shell "-
(5) ibid p.140; Heckwelder, p.205.
(6) cf. Lawson's Hist. of Carolina, pp. 338,339.
(7) See Supra p.59 ; cf. Jones' Antiq. of the Southern In-
    dians, pp. 495-524; Pubs. of Amer. Bureau of Ethnology
    ii, 255,256.

of the small material, were gorgets, necklaces, armlets abd anklets, pins and ear-rings.

Various articles of stone formed a large proportion of the Indian implements. Of stone, the Virginia Indians made axes, hatchets, celts, swords, mortars, mullers, pestles, hammers, smoothing and crushing stones, etc. Picks, chisels, awls, or borers, bet-sinkers, hammer-stones, and soap-stone vessels are to be found to this day scattered over Virginia soil - remnants of her former inhabitants - Grooved axes, scrapers, drills, knives, spear-points, arrow points and discoidal stones (chung ke) as well as pipes and various ornaments are also abundant even yet in some localities. Nor, as has been estimated above, did the Virginia Indians remain content with the materials supplied by the section of country in which they made their abode; they it would seem, sought far and wide for finer substances and

mountains through the bands of the Manakins or "gyant-like
(1)
Susquesahannaks". Quartz, chalcedony, slate, steatite, hornblende, dicrite, greenstone and hematite were likewise obtained from the same quarter and manufactured into various articles of utility or ornament.

Fire - that great key to all civilization - was produced among the Virginia Indians much as it was among the primitive Semites of Babylonia, the early Japanese and Chinese, and the Bushmen and the Polynesians of almost our day, that is to say, it was brought about by the friction method. It was kindled by chafing or rubbing a dry pointed stick in a hole formed in a little square piece of wood: in a moment's time, ignited sparks would fly from the point of contact of the two pieces of wood, quickly inflaming any
(2)
dry thing placed near enough. The method of obtaining fire by striking together metals or flints does not seem to have been familiar to the Virginia Indians; some metallic substances were, however, undoubtedly known to them, and they possessed some knowledge of melting and moulding these metals.
(3)
als. Strachey, for instance, speaks of "the Bocootowwan-

---

(1) See in general on the subj.art. on "Distribution of Stone Implements in the Tide-Water Country" by W.H.Holmes in American Anthropologist for 1893; see supra; see also Smith's Gen.Hist.bk.2,p.350.
(2) Smith Gen Hist. bk.2,p.363; Strachey, p.112; Beverley p.182.
(3) Strachey,p.27. This authority mentions "copper" as being mined at the other places.

anks who melted copper [1] and other metals as living to the northward of the falls (of the James) and ending to the north-east." Ralph Lane [2] describes a copper mine up the river Moratoc; [3] Hariot [4] speaks of finding "divers small plates of copper some fifty miles in the mainland and mentions "mountains and rivers that yield white grains of metall, which is to be deemed silver." [5] Newport, speaking of the Blue Ridge (=Quirauk) says: "Here our guide whispered with me that this coquassa (=red-stone=copper) was got in the hills of rocks and between cliffs in certaine veins." Purchas [6] and Richard Hakluyt [7] also mention copper-mines as existing and as being worked among the Virginia Indians. Purchas, in particular, gives us some inkling of how the "Virginians" melted copper. He thus describes their methods:-

---

(1) It would seem that copper was the best known and most valued metal among the Virginia Indians, as among those of whom Lucretius says:
"Posterior ferri vis est, aerisque reperta
Et prior aeris erat quam ferri cognitus usus"-
(2) In Hak.iii, 315. Description of a mine at Chaunis Temoatan.
(3) Moratoc river - the Roanoke.
(4) In Hak.iii, 329.
(5) In Arch.Amer. IV. 6
(6) Purchas IV. 1784 ("Va. affairs till This Present 1624"
(7) Hakluyt's "Epistle Dedicatorie" to his translation of the Gentlemen of Elvas' Story.

"They report also of copper - - - - gathered at the foote of the mountaines, where they dig a hole in the ground in which they put the oare, and make thereon a great fire, which causeth it to runne into a masse, and become malleable. Neither have they any tooles but stones for that purpose"-
(1)

Ralph Lane reports the "Virginians" as saying that they obtained their metal out of the shallow places of a river falling from the rocks; "The maner is this", he goes on to say, "they take a great toube by their description as great as one of our targets and wrappe a skinne over the hollow part thereof leaving one part open to receive the minerall; that done, they watch the coming downe of the current and the change of the colour of the water, and then suddenly clap downe the said boule with the skinne, and receive into the same as much oare as will come in, which is ever so much as their boule will holde, which presently they caste into a fire and presently it melteth and doth yeeld in five parts at the first melting, two parts of metall to three parts of oare"-

The Virginia Indians applied fire to another very important use - the baking of their earthenware articles -.

----
(1) See Hakluyt, iii, 365.

In other words they practised with some degree of skill the art of making pottery - Thomas Hariot,[1] historian of the Roanoke expedition of 1587 gives the following brief but clear account of this industry and its utility among these Indians, illustrating the process by a copper plate which appears in De Bry.[2] He says: "Their weomen know how to make earthen vessels with special cunninge and that so large and fine, that our potters with thoye wheles can make noe better; and then remove them from place to place easeyle as we can doe our brasen kettles. After they have sett them uppon a heape of earthe to stave them from fallinge, they putt wood which being Kyndled one of them taketh great care that the fyre beeme equally rounde both. The" or ther woemen fill the vessel with water and then putt they in fruite and fish and lett all boyle together"-

A good collection of such pottery as is thus described is in the National Museum at Washington, and also in various private collections. It has been and still is found in considerable quantities distributed along the Tide-water rivers and bays in Virginia. The workmanship
----
(1) In Hakluyt's Voyages, iii ; Barlow's account in Hak. iii, p.306; and compare Jones: Antiquities of the Southern Indians, pp. 441-446.
(2) From a drawing execited by John White.

implied by this pottery argues a high degree of skill, much higher than that attained by the northern and western tribes. Moulds, it would seem, were very frequently employed in the fashioning of such articles, but not exclusively; for, in numerous cases, the walls of such vessels were, without doubt, built up by hands in other words, these vessels were formed of numerous bands of clay superimposed one on the other, pressed together and then smoothed down by the fingers; or, it may be, some rude implement was employed for that purpose. As for the materials out of which these vessels were made, it may be said that they varied considerably in quality and consistency; sometimes mere clay was employed, but in most instances, such clay was tempered and its quality improved by pounded shells.

There was no very wide range of shape in these vessels. The pot was the type, and no other ceramic form was attempted at least to any extent. Needless to say such a type-plan is simple; for it is in neck and handles alone, that the pot affords room for variations or artistic finish; and even such slight modifications were rarely attempted. Utility, then, not beauty was the object striven for by the Indian potter, and the sooty surfaces and smoke-blackened sides of specimens of Indian pottery alone clear-

The meagre ornamentation possessed by such articles of Indian fictile art consists exclusively in regular impressions made by the fingers, notted cords or some rough tool upon the clay when in a soft condition. "It is interesting to note", says Mr. W. H. Holmes[1] with reference to the character of this ornamentation, "that the tatoo marks upon the foreheads, cheeks, chynns, armes and legs of the chiefe ladyes of the Chesapeake as shown in John White's illustrations of the Roanoke Indians are identical with the figures upon the pottery now exhumed from the Shell-heaps"-

In textile art - weaving - as in fictile art - pottery - these Virginians manufactured a large variety of articles.[2] Wattled structures for shelter or for trapping fish, mats for coverings, hangings and carpetings, nets for fishing, baskets, aprons and pouches for ordinary uses testify to the skill of the Indian in this regard. The thread or rather cord used in weaving was spun by the women "very even and regularly" out of "barkes of trees", deer-sinews or a kind of grass called Peminaw[3].

A high degree of skill was attained in tanning hides and forming clothing out of them: such clothing is fre-

---
(1) In the American Anthropologist, 1, p.241.
(2) See plate opp. p. 131 of Beverly's Hist. of Va.
(3) Smith's Generall Historie, bk.2, pp. 364,365.

quently mentioned as "beautiful" by the early travellers and explorers. The Virginia Indians also attempted bridge-building. These, however, were very "poore", indeed they were so frail-looking that the English at first sight took them for traps laid for their destruction.
(1)

The musical instruments of the Virginia Indians consisted of drums, pipes, flutes and rattles. Their drums were made of a deep platter of wood, over the mouth of which a square skin was stretched, and at each corner of this they would attach a walnut by a string. These four walnuts "meeting at the back side near the bottom "they would twitch till the drum-membrane to which they were attached was "so taught and stiff", that they may beat upon it as a drumme"- Their pipes were fashioned of thick reeds or canes, and their rattles of small goards or pumpkin-shells: of these, says Smith, they had "Base, Tenor, Counter-tenor, Meane and Treble".
(2)

informs us that "Savages and Barbarians dance their joy and sorrow, their love and hate, even their magic and religion." To such an extent was this amusement carried that Mr. L.H. Morgan(1) informs us almost every North American tribe had as many as twenty to thirty different modes of dancing, and the Virginia Indians formed no exception to this rule. Says Spelman(2) in general terms of the fashion of dancing in vogue among these Indians, "It was like the English Derbyshire horn-pipe, a man first, then a woman, and so through them all in a round, ther is one which stands in the midest with a pipe and a rattle with which he begins to make a noyse, all the rest gigetts about wriinge ther neckes and stampinge on the ground"-

One of their dances was performed in honor of stranger-guests. Strachey(3) thus describes it:- "one of them standeth by with some furre or leather thing in his left hand, and sings with all as if he began the quier, and kept unto the rest their right time, when upon a certain stroak or more (as upon his cue or tyme to come in) one riseth up and byginnes to daunce; after he hath daunced awhile, stepps forth another as if he came in just upon his rest
---
(1) Ancient Society, p.116; cf. Jones "Antiquities, etc. pp. 92-96 and 398-390.
(2) Relation of Va. p. CXIV.
(3) Strachey, p. 81; Campbell, pp. 88,89; Percy in Purchas IV, 1685 and following.

and with this order all of them so many as there be, one after another, who then daunce at an equal distance from each other in a ring, showting, howling, and stamping their feete against the ground that they sweat agayne, and with all variety of strong mymetic tricks and distorted features making as confused a yell and noyse as so many frantique and disquieted bachanalls and sure they will keep stroak just with their feete to the tyme he gives, and just one with another, but with the hands, feet and bodye, everyone hath a severall gesture")
(1)

Expressive of sentiments of love and "dalliance", corresponding in some degree, perhaps, to the modern opera, there was a voluptuous dance performed by the Indian ladies of Virginia. A dance of such a nature was that performed in honour of Captain Smith by Pocahontas and a bevy of "thirtie young Women"- a "Virginian Maske"- as Smith calls it -
(2)

Festivals and feasts had also their peculiar and characteristic style of dance . In this, the dancers forming themselves into a ring, moved around a circle of carved pots set up for that purpose, or else around a fire, built
(3)
----
(1) For a plate of such a dance see p.37 of Strachey.
(2) Generall Historie, bk. 3, p   ; also in Beverley,Hist- of Va. pp. 176, 177.
(3) Howe, Hist. Colls. of Va. p.139 et alii.

in a conveniently large place. Each dancer had his or her rattle upon the head, and the favorite weapon in hand. Having, then, dressed themselves up with branches of trees, or some other strange accoutrement they would go on dancing in and out round the posts, singing a wild and outlandish refrain and accompanying it with all the antic postures conceivable, and he was the hero of the hour who could make the most extraordinary gestures.

(1)

Dances of a religious import, they had also; but a detailed description of such dances will not be necessary as they differ in but slight degree from those already described. Suffice it to say, then, that so great was their passion for this mode of expressing their feelings that in every Indian "town" there was what would correspond to the modern "German Hall". - Beverley who informs us of this fact goes on to say "they have a fire made constantly every night at a convenient place in the town, whither all that have a mind to be merry at the public dance or music resort in the evening". -

(2)

of a friendly, mocking, sportive or religious character.
A marked feature of all these was the refrain. The occasion and subjects of such wild chants were various: in one, Okeus and the other gods are besought to plague the Tassantessus (i.e., the English) in another joy and exaltation is expressed at the death of their enemies. An example of one of this latter kind - the sole "Indian lyric" we have—is given in extenso by Strachey⁽¹⁾. Its refrain is peculiarly wild: one "verse" will give its general character:-

      Matanerew shashashewaw erawango pechecoma
      Whe Tassantassa inoshashawyehockan pocosack.
      Whe whe, yah haha nehe wittowa, wittowa.

Among their games, bandy was in especial favour.
Says Spelman⁽²⁾: "They have beside foot-ball playe, which women and young boyes doe much playe at, the men (more sensible than civilized ones are now) never. They make ther Goules as ours only they never fight nor pull one another downe. The men play with a little balle lettinge it fall out of the hand and striketh it with the tope of his foot, and he that can strike the ball the furthest wins that they play for"- While cards and dice were unknown, they did have a game, Strachey informs us, "like primero⁽³⁾ wherein

---
(1) Strachey, p. 79.
(2) Relation of Virginia, p.CXIV-
(3) Primero = the modern Poker.

they can but obscure and do win and lose; they will play at this for their bowes and arrows, their copper beades, hatchets and their leather coats - (1)

The frequent occurrence of discoidal stones in Virginia, which were used, as we know, only in the chungke game assures us of the fact that such a game was practised by the Indians of this state; and, we are informed by Lawson(2) and Adair(3) that such a game was likewise highly popular among the Carolina Indians. Lawson describes this game as "carried on with a staff and a bowl made of stone, which they trundle upon a smoothe place like a bowling-green made for that purpose"- Their "bowl" of stone was cast along the ground upon its edge like a wheel. This casting of the "bowl" was done by the participants in the game in one order. The Indian making the cast would follow the bowl on the run for a space, then stop and cast the staff as near the point at which he calculated it would stop as possible from its rate of motion. All who were in the game did likewise, and he above staff came nearest the point at which the "bowl" stopped won the game; betting, of course, was indulged in as to the result of the game.

------
(1) Strachey, p.78.
(2) History of Carolina, p.98.
(3) History of the American Indians, p.401 and following.

The learning of the Virginia Indians was, of course, limited and meagre: they, however, it would seem had some knowledge of the art of picture-writing and a crude acquaintance with medicine and astronomy. Says the Rev. Hugh Jones[1] in this regard: "They have certain Hieroglyphical methods of characterizing things; an Instance of which I have seen upon the Side of a Tree where the Bark was taken off. There was drawn something like a Deer and a River with certain Strokes and Dashes; the Deer looking down the River, which we interpreted to be left for information to some of their Straggling Company, that certain of them had gone down the River a Hunting and others were gone different ways". On the authority of no less a man than George Washington[2], we are told that the Virginia Indians, when they wished to make any record, or leave an account of their exploits to posterity, scraped off the outer bark of a tree, and with a vegetable ink or a little paint which they carried with them would make markings upon this smooth surface which would be generally understood by people of their tribes. Rock-carvings, pictographs and other reminders of the "Ancient Virginians"[3] exist to the present day

With regard to "astronomy", Captain Thorpe assures us that he found that the Virginia Indians "had some knowledge of the fixed Stars and had observed the North Star and the course of the Constellations about yt, and had called the great bear Manguakaiau, which in their language signifies the same"-

As among most, if not all, semi-barbarous tribes the knowledge of the "Virginians" as to medicine and its applications to surgery and the healing art was, in some respects at least, not to be sneered at, though, on the whole, it certainly will not enthuse us. The medicine of these Indians consisted almost exclusively of roots and the "barkes" of trees; very rarely was it that the leaves of trees or herbs were employed for this purpose.

to imply a knowledge of the beneficial results of lancing
(1)
in such cases.

Persons who were suffering, then, from wounds or disease among these "Virginians" were treated for all ail-
(2)
ments in one of five ways: (1) by sucking (if a wound or other inflammation) (2) by scarification (if an inflamma-tion); (3) by cauterization (this was brought about by ap-plying red-hot reeds to the seat of inflammation, which had been cooled as far as possible by the application of wet cloths);(4) by the administration of certain herbs, roots, bark or leaves either externally or internally to the pa-tient, and finally (5) by the "sweating-system" of treat-
(3)
ment. These Indians also possessed powerful antidotes against rattle-snake bites, some of these as given by Col-
(4)
onel Wm. Byrd are as follows:-

(1)- Rattle-snake root or Star-grass, which "worked by

Violent Sweat".

(2)- St.Andrew's Cross; this was a "common remedy"-

(3)- Ipecacuana, which was called "Indian physic"

(4)- Fern-root.

Among other herbs and roots frequently employed by
----
(1) Smith, Gen. Hist. bk.2, pp. 364,365.
(2) Cf. Jones, "Antiquities", p
(3) Beverley, Hist. of Virginia, pp. 172-175.
(4) Byrd's Westover MSS. vol. 1, p

the medicine-men were (1) the puccoon and wild-angelica pounded together and mixed with bear's oil; this served as an ointment, (2) Wapieh, a kind of earth of a medicinal quality, (3) Wissacan a sort of root, bruised and applied to wounds and (4) Sassafras, employed as a remedy for syphilis. Of these Wissacan and Puccoon were the most esteemed
(1)
medicines, but a decoction of cassine or ilex yupon was also highly popular both as a purgative and as an adjuvant
(2)
to the healthy action of mind and body. With regard to the real value of the "physic" of the Virginia Indians, Mr. W.
(3)
Morean in a letter to the Bishop of Litchfield says that they "have the best secrets any Physician in Europe might have" and goes on to say that they had taught him how to cure any intermittent fever "in two days time"-

Every spring it was a custom of these Indians presumably to improve their health, to make themselves sick by
(4)
drinking the extract of the root wissocan with water. This acted in an exceedingly drastic manner as a purgative and general cleanser of the system, but so debilitating were its effects upon the system, that three or four days were

For dropsies, swellings and to relieve fatigue a sort of "sweating-system" of treatment like our Russian bath was highly esteemed; and as evidence of their high regard for such treatment, a sweating house and attendant physician was to be found in every town. The process is best described by Beverley (1) as follows:

"The doctor takes three or four large stones, which after being heated red-hot, he places them in the middle of a stove, hanging on them some of the inner bark of oak beaten in a mortar to keep them from burning. This being done, they creep in six or eight at a time, or as many as the place will hold and then close up the mouth of the stove, which is usually made like an oven, in some bank near the water-side. In the meantime, the doctor to raise a steam, after they have been standing a little while, pours cold water on the stones, and now and then sprinkles the over to keep t'em from fainting. After they have sweat

To cure swellings they made use of small pieces
(1)
of touchwood of the size and shape of cloves. These were
inserted into the inflamed spot, then burnt to the flesh,
from whence the pus or inflamed matter was sucked by the
mouth of the physician. These physicians, however, or
"medicine-men" who combined the functions of doctors (or
conjurors) and priests made a much greater use of "charms
to cure" than of medicine. "With their charms and Rattles,"
(2)
says Smith, "and an infernal rout of words and actions they
will seeme to suck their (i.e., their patient's) inward
griefe from their navels or their grieved places"- With
regard to their knowledge, however, it is to be observed
that they made a great secret of it, excusing themselves
from divulging it on the plea that "their gods would be angry with them should they discover such and such part of
(3)
their knowledge"-

It was, however, in their quality of seers and their
acquaintance with the mantic art that these "medicine-men"
were especially prominent and influential; and, in this regard they are especially deserving of our attention. We
are informed that Powhatan was "not meanly (slightly) jeal-
----
(1) Smith's Generall Historie, bk.2, pp. 369-370.
(2) Smith, Ger Hist. bk.2, p.370.
(3) Hariot in Arber's Edition of Capt. J. Smith, p.322.

ous and careful" to divest of their fell import some of the prophicies of his conjuror or priests, inasmuch as they were calculated to be subversive of his "Empire"- One of these "prophicies" was to the effect that a nation should over the Chesapeake bay and utterly destroy the "Empire"- In order to put an end to such dangerous prophicies the old "Emperour", Herod-like, exterminated" all such who might lye under any doubtful construction of the said prophecie" - - - "and so", says, Strachey, "remain all the Chessapeans to this daye and for this cause extinct"-(1)

Another, however, of their prophecies was even more curious and interesting; indeed, to judge by the account of Strachey the accuracy with which it predicted events is not exceeded by any other oracle ancient or modern. Writing about 1612, Strachey gives this interesting "prophesie" as follows: "That they should twice overthrow and dishearten the attemptors, and such strangers as should invade their territories and labor to settle a plantation among them, but the third tyme, they should themselves fall into subjection and under their conquest. It will be needless to remind the reader that such events as this "prophesie"

---
(1) Strachey. History of a Travaile into Va. Britannia. p.101

foretells, literally took place. The Indians did only too truly twice (in 1622, 1644) overthrow and dishearten their English "attemptors", but the "third tyme" these very same Indians certainly did "themselves fall in their subjection"
(1)
Traditions, also, almost equally peculiar those Indians had which were preserved by the priests; but into them it will be needless to inquire.
----
(1) Byrd. Westover MSS. vol.1. p.175.

Chapter IV.

GOVERNMENTAL INSTITUTIONS OF THE VIRGINIA INDIANS.

(1)
Captain John Smith tells us that although the Va. Indians were very barbarous yet their government was of such a character, both with respect to the authority of magistrates and obedience of people, that it excelled the government of many places that would be counted "very civil". The form of this government with its apparatus of cockarouses (2) werowances and cawcaw-
(3)
waesoughes etc., was monarchial and too much of the imperial type; for, says Strachey, "one Emperour ruleth over many kings or werowances", representing his "Imperial Highness" throughout the country of Tsenacomacah. (5)

This "Emperor", a ruler corresponding in many respects to the Hos-sa-ga-gehjda-go-wah ("Great War Soldier") of the Iroquois, was known to the early settlers of Virginia of the name of Powhatan. His ordinary name, however, among his own subjects was Wahunsonacock. The extent of his dominion was wide and the number of his subjects large, con-
----
(1) Gen. Hist. bk.2,p.375; Stith p.34
(2) Is our word "caucus" a survival of this Indian word?
(3) Strachey,
(4) ibid. p.47
(5) Tsenacomacah the name given to Va. by Ind's ibid.p.47
(6) See Smith, Gen. Hist. bk. , p.375; supra, p.
(7) See Supra p.20 for a gen.critique of gov. of Inds.in

sidering the sparse population of aboriginal North America.
(1)
On the South, it extended to the bands of Chowanocks and Mangoags (i.e. the present N. Cline); on the north, its furthest limit was the "pallisadoed town Tockwough at the bend of the Chesapeake bay in latitude forty degrees; south west, a ten-day's journey was necessary to get beyond its limits to Anoeg, "whose houses" says Strachey (2) are built as ours"; to the west, the "empire" extended to the mountains; north-west, its limits were the bounds of the Massawoweekes and "Bocootawwanoughs", unfriendly nations; north-east, the greater part of the Eastern Shore Indians acknowledged his sway.

The "Emperor" Powhatan's chief places of residence were these; his chief and favourite one, when the English first came to Virginia, Werowocomoco (3) was situated on the north side of the Pamunkey river some ten miles from Jamestown in the present county of Gloucester (4); but afterwards tired and disgusted at the encroachments of the English, the old Emperor left Werowocomoco and went to live at Orapakes, situated, "in the deserts at the top of the river Chickahomania betweene Youghtamund and Powhatan" (5) Another

------

(1) Strachey, 48
(2) Strachey, 47 , following Smith, bk.2, p.375.
(3) Ibid. p.17
(4) Stith, p.53; "Newes from Virginia" p.11

favorite residence of his was Powhatan, a locality about a mile below where Richmond city now stands.

With reference to personal appearance, Powhatan is described by Strachey (1) as " a goodly old man and not yet shrincking, though well beaten with many cold and stronge winters - - - supposed to be little lesse than eighty yeers old - - -, with graie haires, but plaine and thin, hanging upon his broad sholders, some fewe haires upon his chin, and so on his upper lippe; he hath beene a strong and able salvadge, synowye, and of a daring spirit, vigilant, ambitious, subtle to enlarge his dominions; for, but the countryes Powhatan, Arrohateck, Appamatuck, Pamunkey, Youghtamund and Mattapanient which are said to come unto him by inheritance, all the rest of his territoryes before named and expressed in the mappe, (2) and which are adjoining to that river whereon we are seated, they resort to have been eyther by force subdued unto him or through fear yielded, cruell hath he been and quarrellous".

Powhatan, then, to sum up, was remarkable as well for the strength and vigour of his body as for his energetic and ambitious mind. He was a conqueror of a savage type

(1) Ibid. p.47.
(2) See Smith's Map. in Arber.

of Caesar and like him, had his provinces and "sub-regulii".
He maintained an absolute rule over his subjects, and like
his "royal brother" James I. of England held to the principles of the "jus Divinum". His subjects esteemed him "not only as a king, but as almost a divinity". In his person he united the supreme executive, "legislative" and "judicial powers. He maintained a savage state and had certain of the privileges of royalty. A guard of fifty or sixty men watched over his personal safety day and night. Regular days were appointed in which all his subjects planted and harvested his corn for him, laying it up in "howses apoynted for that purpose." The principal of these treasure houses was situated about a mile from Orapakes in a wood. It was fifty to sixty yards long and frequented only by priests and in it was stored not only corn but all the "imperial" treasures, viz., skins, copper, paint, beads, arms of all kinds, etc. His wives were many; he had, says Strachey, "a multiplicitie of women", two or more of whom

(1)
(2)
(3)
(4)
(5)

...atan and "then lyving twenty sons and twelve daughters, including Winganuske and Pocahontas"; such of his wives as he "got tyred of he bestowed upon his friends as doth the Turk."

Succession to the office of "Emperor" among the Virginia tribes was through the female line.(1) The dignity descends from uncle to nephew or from brother to brother, e.g. Powhatan's dominions would descend not to any of his numerous sons or daughters, but to his brothers Opitchapan, Opechancanough and Kekataugh and their sisters.( )

The empire of Powhatan for governmental purposes was made up of many subdivisions or "esterns",(?) many of them corresponding to tribal or gentile divisions, some resulting from other causes and the character of the authority exercised by the Emperor and his "sub-regulli" does not, so far as I can judge, present very marked differences from

----

(1) See Strachey, p.43; Smith, Gen. Hist. bk.2, p.376,(A) Beverley, Hist. of Va. p.170; Morgan's Anc.Soc., pp.153-183.
(2) Thomas Jefferson, however, thinks the offices were held in rotation (Notes on Va.p.343) but everything goes to prove that he is wrong. See Lawson, Hist. of Carolina p.195; Strachey, pp.55-63.
(3) Strachey, pp. 55-63;

that existing in many of the other tribes of Southern Indians. Every town or village with its surrounding territory constituted a "shier", and these "shiers", of which there were about thirty-four, were comparatively independent save with regard to the "Emperour", who maintained his authority in them through his "petty werowances" or vice-gerents. There was a werowance or "sub-regulus" appointed for each "shier", and in it he maintained supreme authority, exercising the power of life and death over his subjects, but paying, at the same time, an exorbitant tribute in kind, amounting as it did, as we are told, to eight tenths of all their rude wealth.(1) The territory was thus held, it would seem, by a sort of feudal tenure of the sovereign lord Powhatan; and no such governmental institution as a "confederacy" at least in the general acceptation of the word, existed among the Virginia tribes; for, in every instance, we find the principle of cohesion among the elements of the so-called "confederacies" resulting from fear, not from a voluntary union of independant equals.

Land among the Virginia Indians was held in common, each inhabitant of the different petty kingdoms having equal

---
(1) The names of these Werowances and the extent of their domains are given by Strachey, pp.56-63; Beverley, p.131; and Stith, p.54.
(2) Confederacy equals a union of sovereign states.

rights and hunting privileges; private property, however, in dwellings and gardens was conceded and respected by all. (1) In each of the "shiers" the governmental machinery consisted of four functionaries, and viz. (a) cockarouse or sachem, the Werowance or war-leader, (c) the tribal council and (d) the priests; these must be described in order.

The cockarouse was the first man in dignity and influence in his "shier" or kingdom; he had also "the honor to be of the king or queen's council". One rendered worthy by experience and wisdom was invariably chosen to this high office by the voice of his fellow-tribesmen. He was the highest civil magistrate and had a "great share in administration", presiding as he did over the council, or matchecomico of his kingdom, which frequently convened in the public square of the town. Next in governmental authority to the cockarouse and also a member of the grand Matchacomico of Powhatan was the werowance or war-chief and leader in hunting and fishing expeditions. It was he that led the warriors in war, though in peace his authority was subordinate to that of the cockarouse; still he acted as an off-set to

----
(1) Bev. Hist. of Va. p.178; Archaelogia Americana, IV. p.61
(2) Bev. Hist. of Va. p.131; Smith's Gen. Hist. bk.2, p.377 Cf. the "Pico" of the So. tribes and Lawson, p.195, and Jones' Antiquities p.11.
(3) This office was sometimes hereditary. See Morgan's Ancient Society, p. 170-175.
(4) Beverley, p.179.

the power of the sachem and saw that the "Emperour's" authority was maintained. His appointment was made by the "Emperour" not by his tribesmen (as a usual thing).

There was always a place of council in every town, debating and regulating its individual affairs, and the grand general council house at Werowocomoco ("The Place of Council" par excellence) which regulated matters of general concern to the whole empire. In its deliberations the most profound respect was shown to the "Emperour", bows and genuflexions occurred with startling frequency; a decoction of cassine or the ilex yupon was drunk as a preliminary to solemn deliberations; for such a mixture was supposed to remove all hindrances to clear and exhaustive thought.
(1)
From De Bry we have a spirited sketch of the cockarouse and warriors in consultation.

Outside the matchacomico the relation existing between the cocharouse and werowance on the one hand and the commons on the other was free and unrestrained. These chief men were distinguished from the common herd only by a scalp-lock; they made their own tools and weapons and frequently worked in the fields with the rest. It was rarely that tyranny was exercised by them over their sub-
(2)

such an institution as slavery, however, if not the institution itself existed among the Virginia Indians; for Beverley [1] speaks of "people of a rank inferior to the commons a sort of servants - - - called black boyes attendant upon the gentry to do their servile offices". In the hands of the chief men was also the common store of the tribe; and in their reception of brother werowances. [2] These werrowances, it should be well remembered, could enter into no measure of a public nature without the concurrence of the tribal matchacomico and the favourable opinion of the people at large. [3] When any matter was therein proposed, it was the usual thing for a long consultation to take place between the chiefs and the priests or conjurors, "their allies and nearest friends, and a unanimous decision being reached,

their "manners", their moral sense of right and wrong and
that potent lever of society known as custom, fashion, public opinion, sense of honor or what not. Offences were
punished by contempt, exclusion from society and, in some
instances, by condign punishment. The penalty, however,
did not always "fit the crime," for the Virginia Indians had
no written laws, but like the Spartans obeyed the sanction
of unwritten custom, handed down by their old men; that is
to say, they were in the first of Sir H. Maine's stages of
jurisprudential advance.

By way of recapitulation and summary, then, we may
make the following statements in thesis form as to the organization of the "shier" or dominion of the sub-regulus.

1. Each had a well-defined territory and a name.
2. A few of them had a dialect peculiar to their "shier"
3. Most probably the cockarouse was elected; the werowance was appointed by the "Emperour"
4. Each "shier" had its religious rites, temples, and attendant priests and
5. And in each there was a council of old men presided over by the cockarouse.

---
(1) Jefferson, Notes, p.138; Stith, p.54; Force, 1,p.11.
(2) Strachey, ch.IV. Smith, Gen.Hist. bk.2, p.377.
(3) See supra, p.17 ;
(4) Strachey, p.57, et seq; Morgan, pp.112-121; Jone., Ant.
(5) Strachey, p.82;
(6) Beverley, pp. 178,179; Jones, Pres.State of Va.p.8.

95

In order to give a better conception of the duties of werowance and cockarouse, I have from a study both of the original authorities and of the customs of the kindred tribes gathered, a bit of the duties of each office.

The cockarouse of the Virginia tribes, then, corresponding to the Ha-gar-na-go-war (1) of the Iroquois, had the following specific duties and privileges:-

1- The first fruits were assigned him (1)
2- He had charge of all public and private concerns (2)
3- He presided at the tribal council, and was a delegate to the Imperial Council, (3)
4- His office was for life or during good behavior,
5- His office was elective, though sometimes hereditary- (4)
6- Females were eligible to the office of Cockarouse-
7- Succession to his office was always in the female line- 6
8- There might be several cockarouses to each tribe

---
(1) See Morgan: Anc. Society, p.   ; Strachey, p.51; Jones' "Antiquities" p. 12.
(2) Beverley, p.179-
(3) Strachey, pp. 57-63; Bev.
(4) See Morgan, Ancient Soc, p 170 Strachey, pp. 57-63. "Queen
(5) Smith mentions various Hariot, Smith, Strachey
(7) Strachey, p.62.

The duties and privileges of the werowance, corresponding as he did in most respects to the Ha-sa-no-wa-no (elevated name) of the Iroquois, were about as follows:-

1- He led the warriors in war, having charge of all military affairs-(1)

2- He had the power of life and death (2)

3- He was appointed by the "Emperour" (3)

4- He was the vice-gerent of the "Emperour" and as Imperial legate (cf. Roman proconsul) kept the people in subjection (4)

5- He collected and paid tribute (- 8/10 of all their possessions) to the "Emperour"- (5)

6- He presided over the council of the "Shier" in the absence of the cockarouse, to whom he as a general rule held a subordinate position; but (6)

7- He declared war, and (7)

8- Maintained a rude state- (8)

The priests also played a large part in Indian affairs. Before every expedition and in all deliberations, he was consulted, and never did the werowance determine (9)

----

upon a hostile expedition without his sanction; for, he it was who, like the augur at Rome, could look into the future and foretell the prosperous or unfortunate issue of *stated* a campaign. His chief functions have been summed up below. (1)

Of the general council or Matchacomico of Powhatan, which may be designated the congress or legislature of the "Confederacy", we can ~~with full~~ confidence make the following ~~statements in thesis form~~:-

(1) It was composed of the cockarouses, priests, etc. of
the subject tribes,
 allied (2)

(2) It had the chief authority over the "Confederacy" in conjunction with the "Emperour". (3)

(3) It was open to popular influence, for it (4)
 (a) called together by people,
 was under circumstances known to all,
 (c) open to every one;

(4) It was presided over by Powhatan; (5)

(5) It was, for the most part an advisory body; (6)

(6) It declared war and made peace according to the Emperour's will; ~~(7)~~

---

(1) See infra pp. 127,132.?.
(2) See Hugh Jones' Present State of Va. p.8
(3) Implied in Smith's Gen. Hist. bk.3, p.400-
(4) Beverley, Hist. of Va. p.150-
(5) Smith's Gen. Hist. bk. 3, p.450-
(6) Hugh Jones' Present State of Va., p. 18-
(7) (see note on next page)

(7) It conducted all "foreign relations"(1);

(8) Its action had always to be unanimous;

(9) It managed general domestic affairs.(3)

The councils of the "Shiers" or petty kingdoms corresponded as a general rule to that of the "Empire" mutatis mutandis - Whatever may have been the good government exercised by such petty chiefs over their territories, the Emperor certainly governed in an exceedingly tyrannical manner, if we may trust our authorities. What he (i.e. the Powhatan) commanded, we are told, they dare not disobey; "for at his feate they will present whatever he commandeth, and at the least froune of his brow, their greatest spirits will tremble with fear"-

From what has been already said, then, and a careful study and examination both of the structure and character of the so-called Powhatan "Confederacy" from the original authorities and a comparison with kindred tribes such as the Cherokees on the south and the Iroquois on the north, we shall be justified in stating the main characteristics of the "Confederacy" as follows:-

and this union was the result of conquest in the true
(1)
Roman style of trickery and stratagem.

2- There was a general council of the Confederacy,
meeting at one of the three favourite residences of
(2)
Powhatan-

3- There were also councils meeting in each "Shier" or
(3)
tribe -

4- The tribes, "shiers" or "kingdoms" did not all occupy positions of entire equality among themselves, e.g., Mattapamient, Arrohatock, Youghtamund and Appamatuck, Pumankey and Powhatan were the governing tribes, while the other "tribes" occupied relations subordinate to them, just as in old Rome the tribes of Latium lorded it over the rest of the world, governing therein by proconsuls or werowances.

5- The individual government of every "province" or tribe was carried on by the werowances save in the case of the Chickahominy tribes, which was governed (5)4
by Elders.

6- The cohesive principle of the "Confederacy" was the common fear of the absolute despot - Powhatan, their

---
(1) See Strachey, pp. 55-63; Smith
(2) See Smith, Gen. Hist. bk. , p.400
(3) See Jones, Present State of Va.
(4)
(5) Strachey, pp. 61,62.

(1)
conqueror.

7- The werowances were, in most instances, the deputies or vice-gerents of Powhatan, his children or friends whom he would substitute for rebellious or conquered (2) chiefs -

8- All these tribes paid an exorbitant tribute of 8/10 of all their wealth for the privilege of retaining to some degree at least their separate governments (3) and native sachems.

9- There was no "Salic Law" in Ancient Virginia. Women were frequently advanced to the office of "cockarouse" (4) and attended the Grand Matchacomics.

10- The Grand Matchacomico met upon occasions of public necessity (e.g. war) in the Matchacomico House at Werowocomoco or Pamunkey. It was called together by certain prescribed forms, and had a regular system (5) of parliamentary rules.

11- There was a council-fire of the whole "Confederacy", and two divisions formed in line on each side of the fire, while the "Emperour" sat at one end and pre-

----

(1) Smith, Gen. Hist. bk.2, p.377-
(2) Strachey, pp. 56,57,60,62 -
(3) Strachey, p.181
(4) Ibid., p.56: "Oholasc, queene of Ccraco hansuke" and "Opussoquionuske - - -a werowanqua of - - -Appamatuck"
(5) For the manner of Summons see Strachey, pp.100,101; infra, p.112

sided. On such occasions unanimity was always requisite fo the passage of any measure. Freedom of speech under certain rules was allowed, and frequently great eloquence was displayed.
(1)

12- The influence of the priests was enormous in the government of the "confederacy" and its constituents, and everyone followed implicitly whatever the priest advised.
(2)

These twelve theses embody almost all that can be learned concerning the nature of the "confederacy" of Powhatan; and much the same remarks will apply to the Manakin and Mannahoack "confederacy", whose form of government was most possibly similar if not identical with that of their kinsmen the Iroquois, with whom they a century or so later united.
(3)
(4)

"In Indian Ethnography", says Mr. L. H. Morgan, "the subjects of primary importance are the gens, phratry, tribe and confederacy". The gens, from certain hints thrown out by Hariot and other writers, we are assured existed in Virginia, and our assumption is put beyond a shadow of doubt by the fact that a study of all the closely related Algonkin tribes reveals in every case a division into
(5)

gentes, and usually those of the (I) Wolf, (II) Turkey and (III) Tuttle. Our knowledge, however, in this regard is so very meagre, that we can assert nothing definitely. Nor can we assert anything more definite with respect to the phratry (1) as an organization of the Virginia tribes, though it must certainly have existed. As to the nature of Virginia tribes which are constantly spoken of by old writers, it should be noted that while real tribes existed in Virginia, there were not nearly so many as we might infer and there is a woful looseness in the way the term tribe has been used, for in many cases it has certainly been confused with what should more properly be termed gens or phratry.

In conclusion we should say that the existence of any such thing as a "confederacy" (in any true sense of the term) is not warranted by the facts of the case, and has been shown to be erroneous by the discussion above, for even the ludicrously misplaced term "empire" is preferable and indeed more accurate in describing Powhatan's power, though such a use of the term is clearly a travesty upon Imperialism generally.

When, in addition to our knowledge of the internal

(note (5) on previous page) Hariot, in Pubs. of Amer. Bureau of Ethnology for 1889. p.393 et seq.; Smith's Gen.Hist bk.4, p.570.
(1) Phratry, see Morgan's Amer. Soc. pp. 84-102.
(2) Ancient Soc. p.148

structure of society, we add a knowledge of the tenure and
functions of the sachem and chief, the functions of the
council of chief-man and the duties of the war-chief (all
of which has been attempted above), all that can be done is
complete, and the structure and principles of their governmental system will be known.(1) This is in some form the
statement of that great authority upon such questions - Mr.
L. H. Morgan; and such has been attempted with regard to
the Virginia Indians. It must be admitted, however, that
the data are so vague that little very satisfactory can result from any study, save by aid of the comparative method,
of which of course I have availed myself.

As has been already seen, there were few fixed pen-
alties for crime in Virginia; the will of the "petty kings"
was law in most cases, and so the punishment varied according to the humour of the chief. Certain forms of punishment were, however, employed. We are informed that sometimes culprits were bound hand and foot and cast into a
great bed of live coals, and then left to burn to death:
again, at another time, the head of the criminal being placed upon a stone or altar was crushed to pieces by clubs,
which were wielded by stout savages. In the case of a hei-
----
(1) Ancient Society, p.148.

nous crime, the offender was bound to a tree, while the executioner would cut off his joints one by one, casting them into the fire; then, with shells or reeds, this same functionary would tear off the skin from his face and head, after which, the poor wretch was disembowelled and burnt to ashes.[1]

Capital punishment was meted out in the presence of the chief and his councillors seated in a semicircle, "the victim kneeling in the centre, and the executioner, his left hand upon the back of the criminal, with a stout, paddle-shaped club made of hard wood, striking him upon the top of the head with such violence as to split the skull".[2]

The most cruel and common punishment, however, was to beat with "cudgells" as the "Turkes doe".[3] "We have seene", says Smith,[4] "a man kneeling on his knees and at Powhatan's command, two men have beat him on the bare skin, till he hath fallen senseless in a swound, and yet never cry or complained".[5] For the crime of adultery, Powhatan, we are told, made one of his wives set upon a stone - - - nine days and allowed her food during that time only three times

---
(1) Smith's Gen. Hist., bk.2, p.377; Map of Va. pp.31,32.
(2) Jones' Antiquities of the So. Inds. p.13
(3) Strachey, p.52; Smith's Gen.Hist. bk.2, pp.377,378.
(4) Smith's Gen. Hist. bk.2, p.378.
(5) ibid.

(1) (2)
though he loved her dearly". Says the Rev. Hugh Jones in this regard : "They punish adultery in a woman by cutting off her Hair which they fix upon a long pole without the Town; which is such a Disgrace that the Party is obliged to fly and becomes a Victim to some Enemy, a Slave to some Rover or perishes in the Woods - - - I have been told they have some capital Punishments". The same authority informs us that the lex talionis was recognized to its fullest extent in Virginia, and gives a concrete case illustrating its force.
(3)
(4)

As a punishment for murder we are informed by Spelman (1) that they "weare beaten with Staves till their bones weare broken and beinge alive wear flunge into the fier"; and for robbery the manner of punishment was to be "knowckt on the heade and beinge deade" to have "their bodye burnt".

Before a war was undertaken, the king always summoned his great men or werowances to attend the council. (Matchocoomico) At these assemblies, whenever a war is expected, it was the custom of the young braves to paint themselves black, red or parti-colored (e.g. making half the face red, half black or white with great circles of different hues around the eyes), to don monstrous moustaches and to decorate the body as fantastically as possible. While this paint was yet damp upon their bodies, they would dip themselves in piles of different sized and coloured feathers: these feathers would, of course, adhere to them and would give them a peculiarly terrific appearance. Thus bizarre and bedizened they would rush furiously into the matchacomico and begin the war-dance. Accompanying their steps with fierce gestures expressive of their insatiate

---
(1) ibid, p.CXI.
(2) Strachey (p.100) thus describes the manner of Summons: "An officer is dispacht away, who cominge into the tounes or other wise meetinge such whom he heth to order to warr, striketh them over the back a sound blow with a bastinado and bidds them be ready to serve the great kinge - - - -"

love of vengeance, they would describe the mode in which they intended to surprise, ~~would~~ kill and scalp their enemies, and finally, they would conclude the performance by recounting the past exploits and the ancient glories of their families. After having been decided upon by the Matchacomico, war was declared by different ceremonies.(1) *warfare*

briefly / Their proficiency in the arts militaire and its accompaniments will be best shown by several theses *hereinafter*.

(1) They had officers, e.g., "Capitaine", "Lieutenant", "Serient"- (2)

(2) They employed various tactical orders in battle, e.g., "square order", Quincuncial order, "halfe-moone order", etc:- (3)

(3) They knew the ~~benefits~~ of reserve forces (5)

(4) The warriors painted, and made "hideous noyse" in battle - (5)

(5) Their weapons were bows, arrows, clubs, battle-axes, swords, shields, etc. ~~etc.~~ (6)

----

(1) "Brevis Narratio", pl. xxxiii.
(2 3 4 5) See Smith, Gen. Hist. bk.2, p.368; Map of Va. pp. 72,73.

(6) ~~See Supra p. 67,68.~~

(6) They had a sort of military music:-

   a - Drums,
   b - pipes,
   c - rattles, and
   d - their own "discordant voyces".

(7) War was carried on, ~~just~~ as among the other North American Indian tribes, by cunning, ruse, deception, "Ambuscadoes", etc. The Virginia Indian presents no marked peculiarity in this regard. We are told, that their custom was never to fight in the open fields, but among reeds or from behind trees, slipping out for an instant to discharge ~~their~~ arrows and as rapidly disappearing under covert to fix their arrows upon the string.

(8) In war, they were merciless and blood-thirsty; prisoners were saved only for a death by slow torture, for, they feared that, should they allow any of their vanquished enemies to live, such an one would avenge ~~himself upon them: as a consequence of such suspicions they slew~~ men,

year 1608. Having previously sent some of his men to lodge with these Pyanketanks for the night, Powhatan sent other warriors to surround their wigwams; and, at a given time, these ~~all~~ fell simultaneously upon the enemy, sacking and destroying their habitations. Most of the victims were slain, and "the long hair of the one side of the heads with the skin cased off with shells and reeds they brought away"(1) The men, women and children who were saved alive were presented to Powhatan and became his slaves; and, as a trophy, the scalps of the slain warriors were hung upon a line between two trees.

(9) Besides assemblies for consultation at the beginning of hostilities, the Virginia Indians also employed formal embassies for treating and ceremonious methods of concluding peace (e.g. burying the tomahawk, raising stone-heaps, etc.) (2)

(10) Triumphs and triumphal processions were also popular among the Virginia Indians. As in Ancient Rome, the successful Indian Chief was welcomed on his return home with processions and rejoicings. (3)

The wars of these "Virginians" were by no means few,

but for women and revenge. They were carried on, for the most part, against the nations inhabiting the "westerly Country" beyond the mountains or at the head of the ravines - the Massawomecks,(1) and in a lesser degree the Manakins and the Hannahocks - These Massawomeckes, according to Strachey,(2) dwelt beyond the mountains "from whence is the head of the river Potowomeck - - - upon a great salt-water which may be some part of Canada, some great lake or some inlet of the Sea, and may fall into the western ocean- - - These Massavoneckes are a great nation and very populous, for the inhabitants of the head of all the rivers especially the Patowomeckes, the Pawtuxents, the Susquehanoughs, the Tockwoughs - - - are constantly harassed and frightened ny them, of whom the said people greatly complained"- So greatly, indeed, did those Massawomecks harass and destroy the tribes nearest them that we are told they offered "food conduct, assistance and continuall subjection" to the English if they would protect them from their dreaded foes.(3)

In the ordinary relations of one werowance with another much ceremonious formality and scrupulous politeness is to be noted - their hospitality was in more than one

---
(1) Smith's Gen. Hist. bk.2, p.367. et alii.
(2) Strachey, p.104
(3) Smith's Gen. Hist. bk.2. p.377.

sense truly "Old Virginian". On the news of the approach
(1)
of a famous guest, the king or queen with their retinue
would march out of their town to meet him, carrying with
them all the provision they could think of for his accommodation.
The first thing that occurred upon the meeting
(2)
of the friends was smoking of the peace-pipe, a custom
common to all North American Indians, the sanctity of
which none would violate. After this preliminary, and taking
their seats right opposite one another, each in turn,
hosts and guests would make speeches, accompanied with such
gestures and contortions of the whole body that they would
all break into a most violent perspiration, and become so
breathless as not to be able to speak above a whisper. Indeed
such was the extravagance of their actions that one
ignorant of their customs would have inferred that they
were utterly crazed. A dance of welcome was the next thing
in order, then refreshments were brought forth and indulged
in till bed-time came, when the happy guests would be led
to their quarters, and there welcomed by "two of the most
beautiful Virgins of the town".

------

(2) The peace-pipe was a safe-conduct, a passport, and a badge of the legislative office. See Beverley, pp. 140-145 ; cf. Longfellow's Hiawatha.
(1) Beverley, Hist. of Va., pp. 143-148.

In the great matchacomico of the nation, such gravity and dignity were observed as would not have disgraced the Roman Senate in its palmiest days. Nor was the impressiveness or solemnity of such assemblages due to any grandeur of architecture or elegance of costume, for the council house was generally but the ordinary "long house" and the councillors but dirty savages wrapped in equally dirty skins and blankets. The effect was produced solely and exclusively by the order, decorum and eloquence then displayed.
(1)
One instance of the strict maintenance of such order and decorum is well illustrated by an instance recorded in
(2)
the pages of Beverley. It occurred during Bacon's Rebellion when a deputation of Indians was sent to treat with the English in New Kent county. While a speaker was addressing the assembly, one of his companions interrupted him, whereupon the Indian who was speaking immediately snatched his tomahawk from his belt and split the head of his daring friend. "The Indian", says Beverley, "dying immediately upon the spot, he commanded some of his men to carry him out and went on again as unconcernedly as if nothing had happened".

---
(1) See Speeches of Okaning, Powhatan, Tomocomco and others in South, Stith, Strachey et alii.
(2) Beverley, pp. 178, 179.

By way of summary, then, ~~and to emphasize the statements already made~~, it may be said that primarily the political organization and governmental machinery of the Virginia Indians was, ~~comparatively speaking~~, both crude and imperfect. The different so-called "kingdoms" (i.e., the "Shires") though theoretically governed by the cockarouse in time of peace, and the werowance in time of war, were practically little democracies, wherein the "governors" held but little authority. The principal power was in the hands of the "old men" of the tribe, yet even such "jurisdiction" as they possessed was but slight, for any one could refuse to obey its rulings who pleased.

But when the "Emperour" Powhatan arose and conquered all his neighbors, forming them into subject "provinces", a different state of affairs presents itself. The chief and absolute power now fell into his hands; and, by fear of him and his deputies, the werowances, the whole "empire" was held together. And such "fear" must have been a strong cohesive principle, for during some forty years (circa 1607-1647), the Virginia Indians under the sway of the Powhatan dynasty (1) presented an unbroken and united front against

---
(1) The Powhatan dynasty consisted of the following rulers
        1. Powhatan (circa 1595-1618);
        2. Otiatan (1618-1622);
        3. Opechancanough (1622-1645);
        4. Necottowance (1645-1650(?)).

the encroachments of their English neighbors, and on two occasions (1622, 1644) brought them to the brink of destruction. The influence exerted by the Indians upon the early colonists of Virginia was, then remarkable, and is, to say the least, comparable to that exercised upon their white neighbors by the Iroquois of New York or the Muscoculgees of the South. It should be distinctly recognized, however, that the power wielded and influence exerted by the Virginia Indians was due to the energy and ability of their rulers, rather than to their form of government. On the other hand, however, the government of the Iroquois and the Muscoculgees was quite well developed, and to this fact, not to the special prominence of any one man, are their successes against their white neighbors to be attributed. We should say then, in conclusion, that all governmental ideas among the Virginia Indians were comparatively speaking rather v vague and ill defined.

Chapter V.
RELIGIOUS INSTITUTIONS AND BELIEFS.

In their religion, if we are to believe the reports of the old chroniclers, the Virginia Indians were extremely superstitious and idolatrous. Nor was there any exception to this rule. "There is yet in Virginia", says Smith, "no place discovered to be so savage in which they have not Religion, Deers and Bowes and Arrowes". (1) Every one of the territories governed by a "werowance" possessed its temple or temples and priests or "Quiyoughcosucks", (2) who we are told, was "no lesse honoured than was Danae's priest at Ephesus" In most cases large (frequently 20 yards broad by a hundred long), these private temples" had their entrances always towards the east, while at the west end was a sort of chancel "with hollow wyndings and pillars whereon stand divers blocke imagies, fashioned to the shoulders, with their faces looking downe the church and where within the werowances lye buried - - - and under them in a vault low in the ground, vailed in a matte sitts their Okee, an image ill-favouredly carved, all black dressed, with chaynes of

----
(1) Smith, Gen. Hist. bk.2, p.570; Map.of Va. p.74
(2) Strachey, pp. 82,83.

perle, the presentment and figure of that God". (1) (i.e., Okens).

According to the best accounts the belief of the Virginia Indians was a species of dualism, in which, however, the evil principle received all the worship to the exclusion of the good god, Ahone (2), who, in the Indian logic, did not require to be placated, "because from his goodness he will do no harm"- It was, then, only this Okens, Quioccos, or Kiwasa, the "Devill" (3) who was really feared, for he it was who punished "them (as they thinke) with sicknesse, stirs up the river, and makes their women false to them" (4) and who, says Cooke (5), "was a god that sucked the blood of children - sufficient description!" This dualistic belief of the Virginia Indians is well illustrated by the historian Beverley (6) in a conversation he had with an Indian whom he "made much of" and plied with "plenty of strong cider" to bring him to the point of confidential communication.

------

(1) Quiqoughcosucks = witches says Whitaker. Neill's Virginia Company of London, pp. 278,279.
(2) Strachey, p.83 and Father White's "Relatio" p.41.
(3) Smith's Gen.Hist. bk.3,p.370 & Neill's Va.Co.of London. p.278
(4) Strachey, p.82.
(5) Cooke, p.30.
(6) Beverley Hist. of Va. p.156,157.

From this Indian he first gained some valuable information concerning the idea of God among the Virginia Indians:-

1- That He was universally beneficent;

2- That His dwelling was in the heavens, though his good influences pervaded and ruled the whole earth;

3- That he is incomprehensible in excellence, enjoyed supreme felicity, and

(4) That he is eternal, boundless in perfection, and in possession of everlasting indolence and ease.

After learning so much, Beverley made the pertinent inquiry why, having such a god as this, the Indians should worship the Devil. The Indian answered that it was true that God is the giver of all good things, but they flow naturally from him and are showered upon all men without distinction;- he does not care about the affairs of men nor is concerned with what they do, but lives apart; consequently there is no necessity to fear or worship him. On the contrary, if they did not propitiate the evil spirit, the Indian went on to state, he would "in a certain and inevitable way ruin them, for the evil spirit was ever active in thunder and stormes" (cf. Prince of the

Power of the Air in the N.T.)

The temples of this god of evil, Okee were called Quioccosan, and were surrounded by circles of posts, on which were covered human faces; these posts being reputed as also highly sacred by the Virginia Indians. In architecture, these "temples" were similar to other Indian cabins, except in two great ? that is to say, they were "fashioned arbourwise after their buylding" but had no roof to serve as a vent for smoke. In their interior arrangements they were very dismal and dark; for about ten feet they were cut off by a partition of close mats; this was the place of extreme sanctity - Beverley (1) describes the results of a surreptitious visit made by himself and some of his friends to one of these buildings to gain information concerning them. He found in such a place certain shelves and upon them various mats Each was rolled up and sewed fast. In one of these he found some great bones, in another some Indian tomahawks. There was also found "something which we took to be their idoll. It wanted piecing together". When set up, it would represent an idol of wood, evil-favouredly carved, the Okee, Quioccos or Kiwasa of Smith, who also gives it as his opinion that this god was none
----
(1) Beverley, Hist. of Va. p.152,153,154,155 -

other than the "Devill" himself.

The Historian Burke, however, does not believe that Smith, Beverley and Strachey are implicitly to be relied on in the above description of Okee. His opinion is that, had there been any foundation in fact, some traces would assuredly have been found among the neighboring or kindred tribes who later migrated west. Beverley, however, with regard to the idea held concerning the Okee says, "they (i.e., the Indians) do not look upon it as one being; but reckon there are many of the same nature"; and he goes on to state that they like the Greeks, believed there were tutelary deities in every town"; By such statements as these Beverley unconsciously proves that his report is correct;

---

(1) See pl.xxi. of De Bry in "Brevis Narratio". The explanation of the plate is as follows: "Idolum habent nullius regionis incolae Kiwasa appellatum, e ligno trunco elaboratum, quatuor pedes altum cuius caput Floridae incolarum capita refert; facies carneo colore depicta est, pectus albo, reliquum corpus nigro, crura etiam pictura alba variegata, e collo torques pendent sphaerulis albis constantes, quibus intermixtae sunt, aliae teretes ex aere, magis ab illis aestimatis, quem aureum vel argenteum - - - Bina interdum habent in templis huiusmodi idola, nonnunquam tria, non plura quae in obscuro loco sunt reparata, Lorrea ia apparent. See also Purchas. V. 843.
(2) Burke, Hist. of Va. III. pp. 57,58.
(3) Beverley, Hist. of Va. p.155.
(4) Byrd. Hist. of the Dividing Line, in Westover MSS. vol 1. p.105

for we find, upon examination of the kindred tongues that
"oki" among the Algonkins just as "superi" among the Latins
signifies primarily "above" and so "those who are above", i.e.
the gods.(1) In other words the religion of the Virginia
Indians was a polytheistic development of Sky-worship.

(2)
Strachey gives ~~quite~~ an account of the tenets of
the Indians dwelling near the Potomac river. He says that
in the year 1610 about Christmas, Captain Argall was trading with Japosaws "King of Potowomecke" and one day, when
the vessel was lying at anchor before one of the Indian
towns of those parts, "King Japasaws came on board. While
sitting before the fire on board the ship the conversation
happening to turn upon religion and the creation of the
world, the "King" through Spelman as interpreter gave Argall and his companions an account of such customs of the
Indians as follows:

and with what kind of creatures, and yt is true (said he)
that at length he devised and made divers men and women and
made provision for them, to be kept up awhile in a great
bag. Now there were certayne spirits, which he described
to be like great geants which came to the hare's dwelling
place (being toward the rising of the sun) and had perseverance of the men and women which he had putt into that
great bagge, and they would have had to eat, but the goodlie
have reproved those canyball spirits and drove them avaye.
This is a rather vague statement, but Strachey goes on to
say that the boy-interpreter was afraid to ask the old
chief too many questions, so the old man went on telling
how the god-like hare made the water and the fish therein,
and the land and a great deer which should feed upon the
land. The four other gods being envious at this, assembled
together from the North, South, East and West, killed the
deer with hunting-poles dressed him and after they had
feasted upon him, departed again to the North, South, East
and West; at this juncture, the other god, "in despite
for this their mallice to him", took the hairs of the slain
deer and opened them on the earth with many powerful words
charms whereby every hair became a deer. Then he opened the
great bag in which the men and women were, and placed them

the world took its first beginning."

When questioned as to what became of his people after death, the old chief answered "how that after they are dead here they goe to the top of a high tree, and then they spie a faire plaine broad path-waye, on both sides whereof doth grow all manner of pleasant fruits and mulberries, strawberries, plombes, etc. In this pleasant faith they rune toward the rising of the sunne, where the godly hare's house is, and in the mid-way they come to a house where a woman-goddesse doth dwell, who hath alwaies her doores open for hospitality, and hath at all tymes ready-drest green us kata homen and pocohicora,[1] together with all manner of pleasant fruicts, and a readynesse to entertayne all such as doe travell to the great hare's house; and when they are well refreshed, they run in their pleasant path to the rising of the sun, where they fynd their fore-fathers lyving in great pleasure in a goodly field where they doe nothing but daunce and sing, and feed on delitious fruicts with that great hare who is their great god; and when they have lyved there till they be starke old men, they saye they dye likewise by turns and come into the world againe." From the above account, then, it is evident that the Vir-

---
(1) Supra, p. 22

ginia Indians, like many other tribes the world-over, had their own peculiar theories of cosmogony and the origin of man. The "Great Hare" of whom Japazaws speaks was, we find from comparative study, no other than the great culture-hero of the Algonkins generally. He it was who taught them the tillage of the soil, the properties of roots and herbs, the art of picture writing, the secrets of magic,- the founder, in fine, of all their political and religious institutions. After ruling long upon the earth as their governor and king, he finally vanished mysteriously to return again, however, when especially needed.(1) For, just as the Germans had as their legendary hero Frederick Barbarossa, the French Charlemagne and the Britons King Arthur, so all the Algankin tribes have their Manibozho or Michabo,(2) the "Great Hare"; and Strachey's account evidently indicates that the Virginia Indians held such a belief also. In other words, the "Great Hare" of his account is none other than this Manbozau, Michabo or Shawandase.

This divinity appears under different aspects in their different legends. Now he is a malicious mischief-maker, full of wiles and tricks, cunning and

---
(1) D.G.Brinton: Myths of the New World. p.160
   See Schoolcraft, V. p.420 Charlevoix, Relation de la
(2) Nouvelle France. vol. 1, p.93.

crafty, - a sort of Robin Good fellow. Now, as in the above legend, he comes before us as a culture-hero, mighty and beneficent, whose character it is a pleasure to delineate; for he appears as the patron and founder of the occult arts, the great hunter, the inventor of picture-writing, the ruler of the winds, and even as the creator of the world, the sun and the other heavenly bodies.(2)

In the autumn, the "moon of falling leaves", it was he, who composing himself for his winter's nap, filled his great pipe and took a "god-like smoke". Balmy, fragrant clouds of this floating away over the vales, hills and woods, fill the air with the dreamy soft haze of Indian summer. the "Shawondase fat and lazy" of Longfellow

"Had his dwelling far to Southward

In the drowsy, dreamy sunshine,

In the never-ending Summer"

it was from

"- - -the smoke ascending

Filled the sky with haze and vapor,

Filled the air with dreamy softness

Gave a twinkle to the water.

---
(1) Probably in this character he was confused with Okee
(2) Cf. Strachey's Account given above. pp. 101,102.

"Touched the rugged hills with sunshine

Brought the tender Indian-Summer

To the melancholy North-land,

In the dreary Moon of Snow-shoes."

It may seem ~~exceedingly~~ strange that such an insignificant creature as the hare should have received such honour and reverence. Such a curious fact, however, may be due to a natural error in etymology; that is to say, the name Manibohzo and its dialectic varieties, whose component ~~apparently~~ connote the meaning "Great Hare" may very probably ~~have the~~ meaning "Great Light" equivalent to "Spirit of the Dawn" or the East. The "great hare" of Strachey's account will rather be, then, the "great white one" an impersonation of the Dawn or Light, ~~and~~ identical with the Ioskeha of the Iroquois, the Viracocha of the Peruvians and the Quetzalcohuatl of the Aztecs.

(1)

the creation of the world. Afterwards they (i.e. the gods) fashioned the sun, moon and stars, and out of the water as a primordial element "all diversitie of creatures that are visible and invisible." In regard to the origin of man these belief was that woman was first made, and she by one of the gods brought forth children, but at what period or epoch of the genesis this occurred they professed ignorance; the representations of these gods were little images called
(1)
Kewasawok.

All the Virginia Indians were firm believers in the
(2)
immortality of the soul. When life departing from the body, according to the good or bad workes it hath done, it is carried up to the Tabernacles of the Gods to perpetual happiness, or to Popogusso, a great pit: which they think to be at the furthest points of the world where the Sunne
(2)
sets, and there burne continually". Strachey informs us that it was one of their tenets that "the common people
(3)
shall not live after death; "but" says he, "they thinke that their werowances and priests when their bodyes are laid in the earth, that that which is within shall goe beyond the mountaynes, and travell to where the sunne setts

---
(1) See Smith's Gen. Hist. Bk.2, p.374; Strachey, p.96; Beverley, pp. 157,158, etc.
(2) Hariot in Hakluyt iii. p.336.
(3) Says Smith in this connection (Generall Historie bk.2, p.374) "They thinke that their Werowance and Priests

into most pleasant fields, grounds and pastures where yt shall doe no labour; but stuck finely with feathers and painted with oyle and puccoons, rest on in quiet and peace, and eat delicious fruits, and have store of copper, beades and hatchets; sing, daunce and have all variety of delights and enjoyments till that they waxe olde there as the body did on earth, and then yt shall dissolve and die, and come into a woman's womb againe, and so be new borne into the world". (1)

   Metempsychosis, then or the Transmigration of souls, (2) was one of the beliefs of the Virginia Indians, and a firmly rooted one to. That such was the case is indicated by the extreme care paid by them, as by the Ancient Egyptians, to embalming; moreover, it is still further evidenced by a curious belief, wide-spread among them alluded to by Beverly------

which they also esteeme quiyoughcosoughes, when they are dead, doe goe beyond the mountaines towards the setting of the sunne, and ever remaine there in forme of their Okee, with their heads painted with oyle and Pocones, finely trimmed with feathers, and shall have beads, hatchets, copper and tobacco, doing nothing but daunce and sing, with all their Predecessors.

  But the common people they suppose shall not live after death, but rot in their graves like dead dogs".

(1)   Strachey, p.28.
(2)   Ibid. p.98.

ley. This historian tells us that the Virginia Indians reverenced greatly a little, solitary bird which, singing only at nightfall in the woods, uttered the note Powcorance continually, for, these "Virginians" believed that to this little bird the souls of their princes passed, and consequently they would not do it the least injury. A story had currency among them which greatly increased their awe of this little creature. It was to the effect that upon one occasion a daring Indian had killed one of these birds, but the sacrilegious act cost him dear, for he disappeared in a little while thereafter and was never more heard of.
(1)

(2)
Colonel William Byrd gives a very quaint and interesting account of the religious beliefs of the Virginian Indians. The information was obtained from an Indian guide when he was engaged in surveying the dividing line between North Carolina and Virginia. According to this account the Indians believed that there was one supreme God and several "subaltern" deities under him. This Master-god made the world a long time ago. He told the moon, the stars their business in the beginning, which they have faithfully performed ever since. This same power keeps all things in the
-----
(1) Beverley, Hist. of Va. pp. 168,169, 170.
(2) Hist. of Div.Line in Westover MSS. 1, pp.105,110. cf.
(3) Beverley, P. 157.

place
~~method and manner~~. That God created many worlds previous to the present one but had destroyed them ~~for~~ the Dishonesty of the Inhabitants"- This God is very just and very good, and takes the good into his protection, "makes them rich, fills their Bellies plentifully, preserves them from sickness"- As for the wicked, he never fails to punish them with sickness, poverty and hunger; and "after all that suffers them to be knockt on the Head and scalpt by them that fight against them"-

After death both good and bad are conducted by a strong guard into a great wood. They travel together for some time; at length their roads part, one of which is level, the other stony and mountainous. At this point the good were separated from the bad by a flash of lightening, ~~and~~ the good went to the right, the bad to the left. The right hand road led to a "charming warm Country" where "Spring is everlasting" and "every month is May". The people there are always in their youth; the women are as brisk as stars and ~~what is even better~~ "never scold". In this happy place are Deer, Turkeys, Elks and Buffaloes innumerable, per~~fe~~ctly fat and gentle, and trees loaded with fruit throughout the four seasons. The soil there brings forth

At the entrance to this blessed land sits a venerable old man on a mat who examines strictly all that are brought before him, *If* they have behaved well the guards are advised to open the crystal gate, and let them enter the "Land of Delights".

On the other hand, the path to the left leads to a dark and dismal country by a rugged and uneven path. Here it is always winter. The ground is covered with snow all the year and nothing is to be "seen upon the trees but icicles". The people are always hungry, yet have not a morsel to eat except a kind of Patch that "gives them the Dog-gripes". Here all the women are old and ugly, having claws like a Panther, with which they "fly upon the men that slight their passion - - - - they talk much and exceeding shrill, giving exquisite pain to the Drum of the ear, which in that Place of Torment is so tender that every Sharp Note sends it to the quick."

At the end of this path sits a dreadful old woman on a monstrous Toad-Stool, *Her* Head is covered with Rattle-snakes. *She has* gloomy white Eyes, that strike a Terror unspeakable to all that behold her. This bag pronounces Sentence of Woe upon all the miserable

Harpies to fly with them to the place above mentioned. Here they are tormented for awhile according to their deserts. Then they are brought back into the world to see if they will "mend their manners" and merit a place the "next time in the Region of Bliss".

- (1) *thus*
The Indian religion thus contained the three great

were laid in an orderly manner with their rude wealth at
(1)
their feet, upon a large shelf raised above the floor of
the rude building which constituted their sacred Mausoleum.
Here the mummies were watched over by a priest, who kept
the fire burning before them. Near them also was always a
quioccos or idol to keep watch and ward.
          (2)
    The Historian Beverley gives quite a minute account
of the Virginia Indian's method of embalming. "First, says
he, "they neatly flay off the skin as entire as they can,
slitting it up the back; then, they pick off the flesh from
the bones as clean as possible, leaving the sinews fastened
to the bones, that they may preserve the joints together;
then they dry the bones in the sun, and put them into the
skin again which, in the meantime, has been kept from drying or shrinking; when the bones are placed right in the
skin, they merely fill up the vacuities with a very fine
white sand. After this, they sew up the skin again and the
body looks as if the flesh had not been removed. They take
care to keep the flesh from shrinking by the help of a
little oil or gum, which will save it from corruption.

    "The skin being thus prepared they lay it in an
--- ---
(1) Brown, Genesis of the United States, 1, 347.
(2) Beverley, Hist of Va., pp. 169,170. Cf. Spelman's
    (p.cx)dscr. of "ye fation of ther buriall if they dye."

apartment for that purpose, upon a large shelf raised above the floor - - - - the flesh they lay upon hurdles in the sun to dry, and when it is thoroughly dryed, it is sewed up in a basket and set at the feet of the corpse to which it belongs." In the burial of the commonalty, a deep hole was dug in the earth with sharp stakes; the bodies were wrapp't in skins and mats, they were placed (1) upon sticks, and covered with earth. After the interment, the women painted themselves all over with black coal and oil and sat twenty four hours moaning, lamenting.

The most sacred place in Virginia was Uttamussac at Pamunkey near the palace of the "Emperour" Powhatan. Here, (2) upon the top of "certaine redde sandy hills in the woods" rose their great temple, their "chief holie house", near it were two other temples sixty feet in length. All of them fitted with "images of their kings, and Divells and Tombes of their Predecessors". Such sanctity was ascribed to this locality that no one but the priests and kings could enter it. Here the priests held con-
----
(1) See also Jones' Present State of Va., p.16; Smith's Generall Historie. bk.2. p.391; Strachey, pp.89,90.
(2) Smith's Gen. Hist. bk.2, p.371

(1)
ferences with their gods and delivered oracles; and such was the extreme veneration in which such oracles were held that the "simple laytie would doe anything how despotic so-
(2)
ever that was commanded them", and furthermore, they durst not go up the river near by unless they previously cast some peece of copper, white beads or Pocones" into the water "for feare that Okeus should be offended and revenged of them" At this place, also, officiated seven priests of whom the chief one alone was distinguished by ornaments, while it was only in a very slight degree that the inferior
(3)
priesthood differed at all from the commonalty.

The chief-priest wore upon his shoulders a middle-sized cloak of feathers, "much like" we are told,"the old sacrificing garment which Isidorus calls cassiola"; and his head-gear was especially conspicuous and unique. It was
----
(1) "As I learned" says Purchas (V, 343),"that their Okeus doth often appear to them in this House or Temple; the manner of which apparition is thus: First, four of their Priests or Sacred Persons goe into the House, and by certaine words of a strange Language-call or coniure their Okeus, who appeareth to them out of the air, thence coming into the House and walking up and down with strange words and gestures, causeth eight more of the principal persons to be called in all which twelve standing around him, he pronounces to them

made as follows: Some twelve or sixteen or even more snakes skins were stuffed with moss, and also as many weasel and other skins. All these were tied by the tails, so that they met at the top of the head like a "large tassell", around which was a coronet of feathers, while the skins hung down round the face, neck, and shoulders in such a way as to hide it almost entirely. The priest's countenance was always painted in a grim fashion; his chief emblem of office was the rattle; and the chief devotional exercise consisted, of weird songs or "hellish cries", in the rendition of which, one acted the part of precentor. His program was, on occasions, varied by an invocation "with broken sentences, by starts and strange passion, and at every pause the rest of the priests gave a short groane." (1)

The most usual costume of the Virginia Indian priest was as follows: A cloak made in the form of the feminine petticoat, fastened, not as we might expect, a out the waist, but gatherings about the neck and tied over the left shoulder, leaving one arm always free for use. This cloak hung even at the bottom, reaching in no case further than the middle of the thigh. This robe was made of the

----
Notes 2 & 3 previous page) (2) S........., k. 2, p. 371. Hist. of Virginia, p. 75. (3) Ibid. p.372.
(1) Ibid.

skin dressed-soft with the fur on the outside and reversed; consequently, when the robe had been worn but a little while, the fur would fall out in flakes. The Indian priests' hair was dressed in an extraordinary manner. It was shaven close except for a thin crest, which stood bristling up like the comb of a cock, running in a semi-circle from the crown of the head backward to the nape of the neck. A border of hair over the forehead was also worn and this, by its own natural strength and stiffness, stood out like a bonnet a was usually stuffed with grease and painted. (1)

Hariot, in speaking of the priests, says "whatever substitute be ever in the werowances and Priests; this opinion worketh so much in the common sort, that they have great respect unto their governors". He, moreover, goes on to say that in their religion "they were not so sure grounded, nor gave such credit, but through conversing with us, they were brought into a great doubt of their owne and no small admiration of ours". In their "great simplicitie" also, they considered the " Mathematicall instruments" of the English to be the work of God rather than men. (3)

---
(1) Howes' Hist. Coll. of Va. p.137.
(2) Hariot, in Huklay, v.III, p.338, et seq.
(3) Spelman, Relation of Va. pp.cix, cx Cf. Lawson's Hist. of Carolina, pp.

The manner of treating the sick does not give us a very
favorable impression of their
(1)
knowledge or skill.

"When any be sicke among them ther priest cums into
the party, whom he layeth upon a mat. A bowl of water is
then set upon the ground between the physician and the sick
person with a rattle by it. The priest kneelinge by the
sick mans side dipps his hand into the bowle, which taking
up full of water, he supps it into his mouth spowting it
out againe, uppon his owne arms, and breast, then takes he
the rattle and with one hand takes that and with the other
he beates his breast, making a great noyes, which having
dunn he easelye Riseth, (as loth to wake the sicke) bendinge
first with one legge, then with the other, and beinge now
got up easelye goeth about the sicke man, shaking his Rattle very softly over all his bodye; and with his hand he

(2) he had a "great share in government" and in "all public and private affairs,"(1)

(3) he had personal conference with invisible spirits,

(4) He propitiated the elements by charms and incantations-

(5) He foretold events, apparently having the power of second sight;

(6) He possessed all the knowledge of the race, whether religious, physical or moral,

(7) He spoke an esoteric language and was the physician of his tribe; finally, the priests were of different grades, some of greater importance than others. The chief priest, for instance, had especially great influence, and on his death, the whole community or tribe united in paying him reverence and celebrating the event with due honors.

When any notable accident or encounter had taken place in wood or wilderness, "certain altar-stones" called by the natives "Pawcorance" were set up, much after the Hebrew fashion. Each one of these stones had its history, which was told to any one desiring information. These Powcoran-

---
(1) Brevis Narratio. pl.xii (2) Bev., Hist.Va. p.149
also Bartram's Travels,p.495
3 ( ) "Brevis Narratio pl. x
4 ( ) C.Jones Ant. So.Ind.

thus furnished the best records of antiquity to the Virginis Indians, and upon them, it was the custom to offer "bloud, deer-suet and Tobacco" on any notable occasion, or when they returned victorious or successful from the war or the chase. The chief of the Pawcorances was at Uttamassack. It was of solid crystal of great size, and upon it sacrifices were made at the most solemn festivals. Says Beverley (2) "His soulaientmene nous presuader, qu'ille etait si transparente qu'on pouvait bien voir au travers le grain de la peau d'un homme; et qu'elle etait de un poids prodigeuse".

There seem to have been no set holy days (3) appointed by the Virginia Indians for religious festivals, though there were quite a number of them. The coming of the wild fowl, e.g. geese, ducks, teel, etc., the return of their hunting season, and the ripening of certain fruits, were solemnized as festivals. Their greatest annual festival, however, was that of the corn-gathering, harvest home, at which the revelling occupied several days, together; To these they all contributed as they did to the gathering of
----
(1) Beverley Hist. of Va. 168. Strachey, p.98.
(2) Historie de la Virginie, p.177
(3) Purchas, v. 843.

the corn. On this occasion, corresponding as it did, to the Boos-ke-tau of the Creeks, there was the greatest variety of past times, war dances and boastful songs, to the effect that their corn being at length gathered, they should now have supplied for their families and so there will be nothing for them to do but go to war, travel, or seek new adventures.(1)

A second annual festival. It with a fast of the severest nature. Then came a feast, the old fire was put out, and by the friction of two pieces of wood, a new fire was kindled. Sand was then sprinkled on the earth and, to make the lustration complete, an emetic and purgative of cassina was taken by the whole nation. All crimes save murder were pardoned at this festival, and the solemnities were concluded by a funeral procession, symbolic of the fact that henceforth the past was to be buried in oblivion, as evidencing this, criminals having taken a decoction of cassina sat themselves down by the side of the people they had injured with perfect security.(2)

The manner of worship employed at such festivals va-

---
(1) Lowe's Hist. Coll's of Va. p.139 - cf. Jones "Antiq. of the Southern Indians. pp. 99,100.
(2) Purchas, His Pilgrimes, v 839

ried; sometimes, they made a large fire in a house, or the fields, and danced around it, sometimes a man or some of "the fayrest Virgins of the companie", in the midst they would dance and sing around them, while these latter in the meantime "as yt were turned about in their dancinge" and clapped their hands. After all such ceremonies, feasting was in order. Solemn dances were likewise performed in remembrance of the dead (1), for deliverance from some great danger, or on the occasion of a return from war. safe and sound.

Among the Virginia Indians there were various kinds of conjurations, or pawawinges (2), one of which Captain Smith observed when a captive at Pamunkey. On this "conjuration" he gives the following account:-

"Early in the morning a great fire was made in a long house and a mat spread on the oneside, as on the other; on the one they caused him to sit, and all the guard went out of the house, and presently came skipping in a great grim fellow, all painted over with coal mingled with oyle,- - - and in a manner covered his face; with a hellish voyce and a rattle in his hand. With most strange gestures
-----
(1) Purchas, His Pilgrimes, V. 838; see also pl. xvii of Hariot, De Bry.
(2) Smith Gen. Hist. bk.3, p.398 in Beverley, p.158.

and passions he began the invocation, and environed the fire with a circle of meale; which done, three more much like devills came rushing in with the like antique tricks, painted halfe blacke, halfe red, but all their eyes were painted white and some red stroakes like mutchato's along their cheekes; round about him these fiends danced a pretty while and then came in three more as ugly as the rest; with red eyes; and white stroakes over their blacke faces, three of them on the one hand of the chief Priest, three on the other. Then all with their rattles began a song, which ended, the chief Priest layd down five wheat cornes; then strayning his arms and hands with such violence that he sweate, and his veynes swelled, he began a short Oration: at the conclusion they all gave a short groane; and then layd down three graines more. After that, began their song againe, and then another Oration, ever laying downe as many cornes as before till they had twice incircled the fire: that done they tooke a bunch of little sticks prepared for that purpose, continuing still their devotion and at the end of every song and oration, they layd down a stick betwixt the divisions of corne. Till night, neither he nor they did eat or drink; and then they feasted merrily with the best provision they could make. Three days they used this Cer-

emony") The meaning of it all, they told him, was to find out if he intended them well or ill. The circle of meal signified their country; the circles of corn, the mounds of the sea; and the shells his country. They imagined, we are told, that the earth was flat and round, considering themselves as occupying its centre -) a belief common to all savage cosmogonies.

The conjuror was the friend and ally of the priest, or frequently the same person was both conjurer and priest. When in the act of conjuration, the conjuror, usually a black bird with extended wings fastened to the ear, seemed to be seized with a divine madness and assumed an air of frenzy and quick movement contorting himself into various convulsive postures -/All his faculties seemingly in the highest state of tension.
(1)
(2)
Hariot says of these Virginia conjurors: "They be verye familiar with devils, of whom they enquire what their enemyes doe, or other suche thinges. They shave all their heads savinge their creste which they weare as others doe, and fasten a small blacke birde above one of their eares

skinne - - They weare a bagg by their side. The inhabitants give great credit unto their speeche, which oftentimes they finde to be true." Such, indeed, was the esteem and veneration in which the conjuror was held that no enterprise was undertaken without consulting him; and such a practice was not without reason, for by their superior opportunities they engrossed almost all the historical or scientific knowledge of their respective tribes, though of course such knowledge was extremely vague.
(1)

One of the superstitions propagated by them was such an one as this: Near the falls of the river James below where Richmond now stands, may be seen, about a mile distant from the river, a rock upon which several marks are imprinted, apparently the foot-prints of some gigantic man. These they were assured were the foot-prints of their god Kiwasa as he walked through the land of Powhatan, A tale somewhat resembling that told by the Ancient Romans of the hoof marks left in stone near Lake Regillus, made, it was said, by the hoof of the horses of the Dioscuri.
(2)
(3)
(4)

Writes Rev. Alex. Whitaker of the "magic and sorcery" of the Virginia Indians "Another accident fell out in

(1) ..riot, in hakluyt, iii, 339
(2) Cooke's Hist. of Va. p.30; Campbell, Hist.of Va. p.80.
(4) Letter to Crashaw in Brown's Genesis of U.S., 1.498,499
(3) Livy II, 19

the march up Nansemond river, as our men passed one of their Towns, there issued out on the Shore a mad crowe dauncinge like Antics, or our Morris Dances before whom there went Quockosite flame and smoke out of a thinge like a censer. An Indian amongst our men seeing the dance told us that there would be very much raine presently, and indeed there was forthwith exceedinge thunder and lighteninge and much raine within 5 miles, and some farther off, but not so much as made their powder damp. Many such Casualties happen as that Principall among them being bound with strong Irons and kept with great watch has strayed from us without our knowledge or prevention. All which things make us thinke that thete be great witches amongst them and they very familiar with the Divill".
(1)

Beverley tells a story confirming Whitaker's account of the sorcery of the Virginia Indians. It runs somewhat as follows: Not long before writing his history he tells us there was a dry time at the head of one of the rivers especially the James near Colonel Byrd's negro-Quarters. Now this Col. Byrd was very much respected and beloved by his Indian neighbors; so one day one of these Indians came to the Colonel's overseer and asked him if the
----
(1) Beverley, Hist. of Va. p.168.

Colonel's tobacco was not likely to be destroyed on account of the dearth. The overseer, of course, answered in the affirmative. The Indian then said he would bring ~~him (i.e. the overseer)~~ rain enough if he would give him two bottles of rum. The overseer promised to give him ~~the rum~~ it if he would do as he had promised. Thereupon the Indian began "pawawing" and apparently as a result of this "conjuration" in less than half an hour there came a cloud in the sky and a plenteous storm fell upon the earth, but only on Colonel Byrd's land and not on any of the farms adjacent. Then, the Indian went away and was not again heard of till the Colonel came in person to the plantation. Then the Indian came back and demanded the promised bottle of ~~"aqua vitae"~~ liquor. The Colonel feigned surprise and ignorance of the ground of the Indian's demand; the Indian with much concern said he hoped the overseer had let him know how he had saved the crop, and in the end the Colonel having made sport of him for awhile, sent him away; but gave him, at the same time, the two bottles of ~~aqua vitae~~ rum.

of medicinal herbs and simples. He would also treated disease by ?

(1) Scarifying the patient's forehead and sucking therefrom, as it were, the "seeds of disease";

(2) Making the patient inhale the fumes of tobacco or other medicinal plants, while lying on his stomach)

(3) Causing the patient to smoke the tobacco 'and
(1)
(5) By mumbling incantations over him

They also conjured for stolen goods, dyed hair, cured toothache, and brought rain and favorable seasons.

Objects of sacred import among the Virginia Indians were various. The carved posts representing human face to be observed, in rows around the Quioccosan were especially venerated. Pyramidal stones and pillars were also adored, not, however, as having any efficacy in themselves to help their votaries, but as symbols of the eternal permanency and immortality of the Deity. Baskets of stones and running streams
(2)
were worshipped for the same reason; though it is highly probable that in the running streams, the Virginia Indians worshipped Manibozho, as the Spirit of the Waters; or, in a less probable degree, they may have adored the Moon-goddess

---
(1) See C. C. Jones' Antiquities of the So. Ind. pp.31, 32,33,34.
(2) Beverley, Hist. of Va. p.168.

who was believed by Algonkins tribes to preside over water, death, cold, sleep, and matter generally.(1)

The conception of holy-water was not unknown to the Virginia Indians, as is evident from the use of it by the conjuror and priests as described by Smith, Spelman, etc.

Another of their observances was their care to keep fire always burning in their Indian dwellings. If at any time the fire went out, it was taken to be an evil omen. If, however, it went out by accident, it was immediately rekindled by the friction method. To prevent any such catastrophe, however, the Indians took great pains to always have in their possession splinters of pine or the fir-tree, which burned with a bright light, so that if one were extinguished others would be on hand to take its place. This curious fact, together with others, leads us to the belief that the Virginia Indians worshipped fire; probably, it is true, not as a divinity, yet as an emblem of divinity.

The Indians of Virginia, however, did not limit their adoration and veneration to images and effigies, they

-----
(1) Schoolcraft, iii. 165.
(2) Such facts as: (a) in the contemporary pictures of De Bry, representing Indian life, a perpetual fire is mentioned as being burned (b) the practice of (mentioned below) casting morsels of food into the fire before eating (c) fire-worship was prevalent among all the kindred Algonkin tribes and Iroquois Septs & (d) Father White says these Indians worshipped corn and fire. pp. 41 and 42.

worshipped also the powers and energies of the material world. When upon the rivers or the sea, the waters became roughened by a wind or a storm, the conjuror would, after many "hellish cries and invocations", cast such things as Copper, Pocones, into the water to pacify
(1)
that god and believing tobacco to be especially acceptable, this was invariably sacrificed and burnt in his honor.
(2)

The fact that the Virginia Indians worshipped a god "angry in storms" goes to prove that there was a worship of the Thunderstorm prevalent among them; a natural worship for the thunderstorm is certainly the "visible synthesis of all the divine manifeststions", the winds, the waters, and the flames.
(3)

Like the Aztecs and Peruvians, the Indians of Virginia (4) sacrificed to the Sun, accounting this heavenly body a god. (5) George Percy tells us "It is a generall rule of these people, when they swear by their God which is

---
(1) Smith Gen. Hist. bk.2, p.371. Strachey, p.90.
(2) See Hariot in Hakluyt, III. p.330, also Jones, Antiquities of the So. Ind. p.396.
(3) D.G.Brinton Myths of the New World, p.150 et seq.
(4) Especially the "Susquesahanoughs" Smith, 118.
(5) Percy in Purchas, 4. 1685-1690.

the Sunne, no Christian will keepe their oat better upon their promise. These people have a great reverence for the Sunne above all things; at the rising and setting of the same, they sit down lifting up their hands and eyes to the Sunne, making a round circle on the ground with dried tobacco; then, they begin to pray, making many Devillish gestures, with Hellish noise, foaming at the mouth, staring with the eyes, wagging their heads and hands a fashion and deformitie as it was monstrous to behold." Furthermore, in his narration, Percy states that William White, who had lived with the natives, told him something of their customs. He affirmed that "In the morning by break of day, before they eate or drinke, both men, women, and children (that be above tenne years of age) runnes into the water, then washes themselves a good while till the Sunne riseth. Then offer Sacrifices to it, strewing tobacco on the water or land, honoring the Sunne as their god. Likewise, they do at the setting of the Sunne".
(1)

From various allusions and notices (scattered) around among the authorities here and there, it is evident that the Virginia Indians adored the Cardinal points and these
-----
(1) Percy in Purchas.", 1630

are to be identified with the four winds, and for this
reason the number "four" was held sacred, and its use was universal among all the North American Indian tribes: and indeed such a belief is a necessary consequence of the hunter's life. Conclusive evidence of the existence of such a belief among the Virginia Indians is given by Strachey (1) who tells how the Indians worshipped the "four wynds" and who mentions four images as being at the corners of Powhatans treasure house, one at each. (2) Purchas also informs us on good authority that the Virginia Indians "worshipped towards a certaine Hoope or sphere doubled in a crosse, which they set upon a heape of stones in this house." The latter however, may be identified with the worship of the great Spirit, a symbol of whom is described by Purches (3) for We are told by Longfellow that Gitche Manito the Mighty" was painted,

"As an egg with points projecting

To the four winds of the heavens".

"Everywhere is the Great Spirit

Was the meaning of this symbol."

------

(1) Strachey, pp. 98,99. Smith also.
(2) Purchas, ". 848.
(3) Hiawatha.

Human sacrifice was frequently practiced by the Virginia Indians. Spelman[1] tells us in this regard: "but upon necessetye yet once(e) in the year, their priest makes a great cirkell of fier in ye which after many observances in the conventions they make offer of 2 or 3 children - -to their god if he will apeare unto them and show upon whom he will have desire. Upon which offringe they heare a noyse out of ye Cirkell nominatinge such as he will have, whome presently they take bindinge them hand and foote and cast them into ye cirkell of the fier, for be it the king's sonne he must be given if once(e) named by ther god. After the ceremonees performed the men depart merily, the women weepinge".

The Virginia Indians, however affirmed that they withdrew their children not because of desire to sacrifice them but to consecrate them to the service of their god. It is, however, an only too well established fact that only a few were reserved to the service of the god, while the rest were all of them slaughtered. Smith[2] gives the following account of the annual sacrifice of children among these Indians as narrated to him by an eye-witness:

----
(1) Relation of Virginia, pp. cv, cvi. Cf. Jones "Antiq. of the So. Ind." pp. 23,24.
(2) Smith Gen. Hist. v.2, pp. 373,374.

"Fifteene of the properest young boyes, of tweene ten and fifteene years of age they painted white. Having brought them forth the people spent the fore-noon in dancing and singing about them with Rattles. In the afternoone they put the children to the roote of a tree. By them all the men stood in guard every one having a bastinado in his hand made of reeds bound together. These made a lane betweene them all along, through which there were appointed five young men to fetch the children; so every one of the five went through the guard to fetch a child, each after the other by turns. The guard fiercely beating them with Bastinadoes, and they patiently enduring and receiving all, defending the children with their naked bodies from the unmerciful blows that pay them soundly, though the children escape. All the while the women weep and cry out very passionately, providing mats, skins, mosse and dry wood as things fitting their children's funerals.

After the children were thus passed the guard, the guard tore down the trees, branches and boughs, with such violence that they rent the body [of the trees] and made

asked the meaning of this ceremony, Smith's informant told
im that not all the children died, but only such a part of
them as fell to Okee by lot, whose left breast Okee sucked
till they died, while the rest were kept in the desert with
nobody with them but the priests and conjurors. Moreover, it was deemed so necessary
~~such was the necessity of celebrating~~ this sacrifice, that
were it omitted, these Indians thought that their Okee or
devil and all the other "quiyoughcosoughs" would give them
no deer, turkies, corns or fish, and other still tribes would make
great slaughter of them.

(1)

The practice of Huskanawing was ~~another extremely~~ a
curious ceremonial usage observed periodically by the Virginia Indians. By it priests were instituted and warriors
first recognized as such.
~~ushered into "life" as it were.~~ Like ceremonies were in
vogue among all the North American tribes. The ~~and such a~~ usage
~~of analogous character is that~~ described by Longfellow as
Hiawatha's fasting. This solemnity of the "Huskanawing"
took place every thirteen or fourteen years or even more

for seven months with hardly any sustenance but the extract of some half poisonous roots, or a decoction of the leaves and the twigs of the cassina or ilex. (poison) As a result of this unnatural fare, madness came on, and the fit was prolonged eighteen days, during which they were closely confined. The place of confinement was called a Huskanaw-pen, "one of which", says Beverley, (1) "I saw belonging to the Pamunkee Indians in the year 1694. It was in shape like a sugar loaf, and every way open like a lattice for the air to pass through." When a sufficient portion of this intoxicating cassina had been taken the "medicine man" candidate gradually diminished the dose; so that in due time they recovered their senses and were brought back to the town.

This process Beverley supposed to act like the waters of Lethe upon the memory. "To release the youth from all their childish impressions, and from that strong partiality to persons and things which is contracted before reason becomes a guiding principle in life. So that when these young men came to themselves again, their senses may act freely without being biased by the checks of custom and education. Thus they become discharged from any ties of
----
(1) Beverley, Hist. of Va., p. 179.

blood, and are established in a state of equality and perfect freedom, to order their actions and dispose of their persons as they think proper, without any other control than the law of nature" (1)

Such then is the existing evidence as to the religious institutions and beliefs of the Virginia Indians; the accounts of the old historians are incomplete but they are all we have. There is enough, perhaps, to warrant the statement that the Virginia Indians had a well developed cult and absolute belief in the efficacy of religious ceremonies. Our Indians were of an extremely superstitious. They saw spirits in religious nature, gods in the elements, every animal, every plant.

(New page)

INDIAN SURVIVALS IN VIRGINIA.

It will not be amiss to notice, in conclusion, some of the Indian survivals in our day.

---
(1) Ibid, p. 180.
(2) Strachey, p. 100

1. Such common words as "pone", "hominy", "hiccory", "tuckahoe", "chinquapin", "persimmons", "barbecue" ~~and "caucus"(?)~~ are all derived from the Virginia Indians.

2. The burial places of these Indians, their shell-heaps, ~~the~~ rock-carvings, and pictographs still remain scattered here and there over Virginia's soil, and their elements, & beads arrow-heads ~~etc.~~ are constantly being dug up.

3. Indians still exist in Virginia. With reference to them ~~all such Indians~~, we should say, however, that there is not a single full-blooded Indian, speaking their native own language from Delaware Bay to Pimlico sound. There are, however, two small bands of so-called "Indians" living, ~~to this day~~, on two small reservations in King William County, north-east of Richmond.

These people, ~~however~~, are of mixed blood. For the most part they are part negro, part Indian. It is still their boast, ~~however~~, that they are descendants of Powhatan's warriors, ~~and un~~ good evidence of their enter present ~~mining~~ ambition ~~in the right direction~~ is an application recently made by them for a share in the ~~school~~ privileges of the Hampton Schools.

These ~~two~~ bands are known by two names; the larger is called the Pamunkeys(120 souls), the smaller band

governed in both instances by chiefs and councillors, together with a board of white trustees chosen by themselves.

Mr. Mooney (1) gives the following interesting account of the present condition of the tribe, written him by Bradly, chief of the Pamunkeys. As given by Mr. Mooney, errors of spelling and grammar corrected, this report reads as follows: "There is an Indian Reservation in King William county, Virginia by the name of Indian town, with about 20 souls. They subsist chiefly by hunting and fishing for a living. They do not vote or pay taxes. We have a chief, councilmen and trustees, and make and enforce our own laws. I am chief of the tribe, W. A. Bradcy. There is a small reservation on Mattapony river. J.M. Allamand is chief"

4. The Descendants of Pocohontas.

The historian Stith (2) notices Thomas Rolfe, son of Pocohontas (Matoax) and John Rolfe and his descendants. "He (Sc. Thomas Rolfe) left behind him an only daughter, who was married to Colonel Robert Bolling;

---
(1) In American Anthropologist, vol. III p.130
(2) Hist of Va., p. 146.

by whom she left an only son, the late Major John Bolling, who was father to the present (1747) Colonel John Bolling, and several daughters married to Colonel Richard Randolph, Colonel John Fleming, Dr. William Gay, Mr. Thomas Eldridge and Mr. James Murray. So that this remnant of the Imperial Family of Virginia which long ran in a single person is now increased and branched out into a very numerous progeny". And so it now appears, as can be seen at a glance in Wyndham Robertson's record "Descendants of Pocohontas", it is not entirely accurate and not include all her descendants at same is are "legion".

5. Indian place-names in Virginia. The following are given principal ones with their meanings in alphabetical order.

Accohanoc (Algonkin) = "as far as the river"; name of a river.

Accomac (Alg.) = "a broad boy" or "the other side-land

Accotuck

Acquia (Alg.equiwi) - "in between something" or "muddy creek".

Alleghany

Aquasco (p. Alg. Achawooguit) - "grassy".

Chickahominy - "turkey-lick".

Chowan = "the South" or the Southern Co[...]

Conecocheague = "indeed a long way"

Cowanesque - "briery, thorny, bushey".

Chesapeake - "a superior, or greater, sa[...]

Kanawha - "river of the woods"

Kettalan = "the great town"

Mattapony - "no head to be had at all". √

Meherrin - "on the island".

Monocacy - "stream containing large ben[...]

Mononghela - "high banks breaking off a
        down" √

Nansemond - "from whence we fled".

Nanticoke - "tide-water people"

Onancock = "foggy-place".

Occohanock - "crooked, winding stream"

Orequon - "a stream of whitish colour".

Ossining - "stony place".

Osso - "white water".

Pamunkey - "in the sweet house where we[...]

Patapsco - "back-water".

Patuxent - "little falls".

Powhatan - "falls in a stream".

Pocohontas - "bright stream between two hills(.) or
    "little wanton",

Pocataligo - plenty of fat ducks".

Poconoke - "knobby".

Pocoson - "a place where balls, bullets or lead is
    to be found".

Port Tobacco - "a bay or cove";

Potomac - "they are coming by water" or "place of
    burning pine".

Pungoteague - "the place of dust" (or powder)

Quantico - "dancing".

Rappahanock - "where the tide ebbs and flows".

Roanoke - "place of shells"

Shenandoah - "the Spruce Stream"-"the stream of

Tuckahoe - "deer are shy".

Tuscarora - "shirt-wearing people".

Werowocomoco - "house of the chief".

Wheeling - "place of the head".

Wicomico - "where the houses are building".

Wyanoke - "the going around place".

Wyoming - "large fields" or plains.

Walla hotoola - "the river that bends".

Youghioheny - "the stream flowing in a circuitous

(1)
~~course.~~

Numerous are ~~the Indian~~ names still in use in Virginia and singularly applicable ~~to~~ ~~are the~~ poetic words of Mrs. L. H. Sigourney -

- - - - their name is i[n] [the] waters -

Ye may not wash it out.

~~and~~ - - - their memory lieth on your hills

Their baptism on your shore.

Your everlasting rivers speak

Their dialect of yore".

6. "Indian Summer" is ~~another~~ a familiar term still ~~in use~~, deriving its origin from the Indian wars of ~~the~~ our Western country. Says Doddridge says, "This expression ~~(se. Indian Summer)~~ has continued in general use, though the origin of the term has been forgotten; still, he goes on, "a backwoodsman seldom hears this without a chill of horror, since he understands the term in its original sense. The settlers enjoyed no peace but in the winter season, when the vigor of the weather prevented Indian incursions. The visit of winter was heralded with delight by the settlers, who in spring and early,

---

(1) This list of Ind. names is from Rochefeller, Schoolcraft
(2) "Indian Names"
~~(3) Notes, p. 10.~~

Fall had been cooped up in the forts and stockades. At the coming of the winter the farmers with their families returned to their homes joyfully at the release from confinement, all was bustle and hilarity. The depths of winter were more pleasant than the month of June to the settlers.

It, however, sometimes happened that after the winter had begun - - - the smoky time commenced, and lasted for a considerable number of days. This was Indian Summer, since it afforded the Indians another opportunity for visiting the settlements - - - ".

BIBLIOGRAPHY OF WORKS USED IN PREPARATION
OF THE MONOGRAPH.

Adair: History of the American Indians, London, 1775 -
American Bureau of Ethnology (Annual Report and Publications of),
" Anthropologist
" Ethnological Society (Transactions of)
Dundas and Barlow's Narrative in Hakluyt's Voyages -
Archaeologia Americana, especially vol. 1V. containing also,
Archer's Account -
Bancroft's History of the United States. N.Y. 1883 -
Bartram's Travels, etc. London, 1792 -
" "Observations on the Creek and Cherokee Indians"
in Trans. of Amer. Eth. Soc. iii, pt. 1, p.39 -
Bartel's Medecin der Näturvölker, Leipzig, 1893.
Beverley's History of Virginia, Richmond, 1855 -
" Historie de la Virginie. Amsterdam, 1712 -
Brickell's "Natural History of North Carolina, Dublin, 1767
Brinton's Myths of the New World, N.Y. 1868 -
Brown's Genesis of the United States, Boston, 1890 — 2 vol
Burk, John Daley History of Virginia. Petersburg, 1804-16
Byrd's Westover MSS. 2 vols. Richmond, 1846 -
Campbell's History of Virginia, Phila. 1860 -
Charlevoix's Relation de la Nouvelle France - 1693.
Churchill's Voyages (Norwood's Voyages)
Cooke's Virginia. Boston, 1884 -
De Bry's Edition of Hariot's "Brevis Naratio"- Francforte
ad Moenum 1590.
" "Admiranda Naratio" Francforti admoenum 1590.
Doddridge's "Notes". Albany, 1826 -
Drake's History of the North American Tribes, Boston, 1834-
Eubank's North American Rock-Writing. Morrisania, N.Y. 1866
Encyclopedia Britanica (Ninth Edition)-
Field's Indian Bibliography. Map, 1873 -
Fiske's Discovery of America, 2 vols. Boston and New York.
1872.
Force's Tracts, 4 vols. Washington, 1836-1846.
Forrest's "Hist. and Description Sketches of Norfolk, 1853
Hakluyt's Voyages, London, 1809-1812 -
Harris' Voyages, London, 1805 -
Hariot's Account in Hakluyt -
Hawkin's Sketches of the Creek Country in Coll. Ga. Hist.
Soc. 111. pt.i, p.75 -

Haywood's Tennessee, Nashville, 1823 -
~~Heckewelder~~ -
Howe's Historical Collections of Virginia, Charleston,
    South Carolina, 1852 -
Historical Collection of the American Colonial Church, ~~ed.~~
    by Bishop Perry, 1870 -
Jefferson's Notes on Virginia, London, 1787 -
Jones, C.C. Antiquities of the Southern Indians, N.Y.,1873
Jones, H. Present State of Virginia, London, 1724 -
Kercheval's History of the Valley of Virginia, Winchester,
    1833 -
Lawson's History of Carolina - Raleigh reprint of ed. of
    London, 1714 -
McCulloh's Researches - Balt. 1829 -
Mass. Hist. Soc. Coll. vol. X.
Morgan's Ancient Society, N.Y. 1877 -
Neill's Va. Co. of London, Albany, 1869 -
Percy's Narrative in Purchas, 1". 1685-1690.
Purchas' His Pilgrimage and the Pilgrims, London, 1628-1814
Pinkerton's Voyages - London, 1808-1814 -
Rau, C. Tauschverhältnisse der Engebornen Nord Amerikas -
Schoolcraft's Archives of Aboriginal Knowledge, 6 vols.
    Philadelphia, 1860 -
    " League of the Iroquois, Albany, 1847 -
Smith's Generall Historie (Ed. Arber's Edition), Birming-
    ham, 1884 -
Smith's Map of Virginia (~~ed.~~ Arber's Edition). Birming-
    ham, 1884 -
Spelman's Relation of Virginia   "   Pirmingham,1884
Strachey's Historie of a Travaile into Virginia ~~Britanica~~.
    London, 1849 -
Stith's History of Virginia, (Sabine's Reprint). N.Y.,1865 -
Van Laet's ~~Beschr. van~~ West. Indián - Leyden, 1630 -
Voyages de Francois Conal aux Indes Occidentales, (1660-
    1699). Amsterdam, 1722 -
Waitz, Anthropologie ~~(Amerikaner)~~ vols. 3 and 4. Leipzig,
    1864 -
White's Relatio Itineris in Marylandium. ed. by Rev. Dal-
    rymple - Baltimore, 1874 -
White's Account in Hakluyt -
Wingfield's Account in Arber's edition of Captain John
    Smith's Works -
  ither's Border Warfare.

Samuel Rivers Hendren, the author of this monograph was born March the 19th, 1872, at Staunton, Virginia. After attending private schools for several years he entered (1885) the Staunton Military Academy, which he attended, taking first honors, till 1889. In the fall of 1889 he entered Washington and Lee University from which Institution he was graduated with first honors three years later (1892). He entered the Johns Hopkins University the session of 1892-3, taking as his major subject History, and as his two subordinate subjects: Jurisprudence (Roman Law) and history of Philosophy with an extra minor course in Economics. He attended the lectures of Professors Adams, Emmott, Griffin and Doctors Vincent and Sherwood, to all of whom he expresses sincere obligations.

During the summer of 1893 he attended the Law Course at the University of Virginia.

www.ingramcontent.com/pod-product-compliance
Lightning Source LLC
Chambersburg PA
CBHW020225240426
43672CB00006B/419